SCOTTISH ANIMAL AND BIRD FOLKLORE

MALCOLM ARCHIBALD

SAINT ANDREW PRESS

EDINBURGH

Published by
SAINT ANDREW PRESS
121 George Street, Edinburgh EH2 4YN

Copyright © Malcolm Archibald 1996

ISBN 0 7152 0714 8

All rights reserved. No part of this publication may be reproduced or transmitted in any form or by any means, electronic or mechanical, including photocopy, recording, or information storage and retrieval system, without permission in writing from the publisher. This book is sold, subject to the condition that it shall not, by way of trade or otherwise, be lent, re-sold, hired out or otherwise circulated without the publisher's prior consent.

British Library Cataloguing in Publication Data
A catalogue record for this book
is available from the British Library

ISBN 0715207148

Cover and **design concept** by Mark Blackadder.
Cover pictures by Paul Turner.
Etchings adapted from J Grant: *Old and New Edinburgh* (Cassell, 1887), vol 1; Samuel Green: *Scottish Pictures* (Religious Tract Society, 1891); and 'The Scottish Annals' from Macfarlane/Thomson: *The Comprehensive History of England* (Blackie & Sons, 1861).
Typeset in 11/13 pt Garamond.
Printed and **bound** in Great Britain by Bell and Bain Ltd, Glasgow.

CONTENTS

Prologue v

1	The Horse and the Word	1
2	The Grey Wolf gaping	8
3	Bran, Don and the Green Dog	15
4	A Drove of Cattle	22
5	Condemned to wander the Sea	29
6	Birds of Odin	35
7	Friends of the Lord	41
8	Creatures of the Hillside	47
9	Lore of the Water	54
10	The Witch's Cat	60
11	The Devil's Breed	66
12	And a Cuckoo brought the News	72
13	A Soo's Tail to Ye!	78
14	Fabulous Beasts	84
15	Horny Golochs and Toddler Tykes	91
16	Bears in the Badger's Ford	97
17	Heraldic Animals	103
18	Travellers and Flying Monks	109
19	Fishing with Enchanted Women	116
20	Animals of the Hunt	122

Epilogue 129
Bibliography 130

PROLOGUE

FOR a developed country Scotland has a surprising volume of surviving folklore. Every glen, every river, every town has a depth of legend with tales of people and personalities, of events, battles and witchcraft, of half-remembered beliefs.

It is not surprising then that this folklore should extend to the wildlife, given the continuing importance of animals to many facets of Scottish life. For example, without the black-faced sheep the hill farms would die with the subsequent depopulation of the uplands; the great fishing rivers of Scotland bring both employment and revenue; shaggy cattle belong very much in the Highland glens; and, of course, where would Loch Ness be without its monster.

If all these, and the omnipresent birds, bring enrichment to our lives, they also provide a link with the past: robins on Christmas cards; Robert The Bruce and the spider; the 'one for Sorrow, two for Joy' rhyme of the magpie – all sit quietly in our industrialised twentieth century, yet all were familiar to our grandfathers, and their father's grandfathers. They help to make us what we are. They bring the soft, cool breeze of nature to our mechanised, computerised age and make us think ... if only just a little.

Malcolm Archibald
INNERLEITHEN 1996

ONE

THE HORSE AND THE WORD

THE men gathered round, their weathered faces merciless, calloused hands gripping the arms of thirteen nervous, blindfolded youths. These were the farm loons, the overworked and hard-used lads who performed the dirty and mundane tasks around the farm.

Silence crushed the farmtoun stable, broken only by the whispering sounds of night, the shuffle of heavy boots through straw and the faint whinny of a horse. Stripped naked by their escort, the loons seemed even more vulnerable and the humour was coarse as they were made to kneel before the senior Horseman.

'Repeat the tender of the oath,' the senior Horseman commanded.

The loons, pale in the flickering candle-light, answered:

'Hele, conceal, never reveal; neither write nor dite nor recite nor cut nor carve, nor write in sand.'

There were more questions and the loons repeated the dire penalties inflicted for betraying their trust, finishing with ... 'and in failing may my body be quartered in four parts with a Horseman's

knife and buried in the sea', the voices trembling in unison, dropping to a mumble at the awful words 'or may I be torn to pieces by wild horses'.

After that the atmosphere relaxed as the blindfolds were removed from one youth and a pen and paper thrust into his hand.

'In case you forget, write down the oath.'

Remembering the consequences, the loon refused. If he had agreed, the iron links of a chain would have crashed onto his knuckles and he would have become an outcast among his peers – remember, '*never* reveal'.

Those who passed the test were invited to join the men in a drinking spree. Bread and whisky, both supplied by the loons, were handed round and the Horsemen jested bawdily as the night hours slid past. The loons took it all in, aware that they were not yet Horsemen, aware that they did not know the lore of the horse – very aware that they did not have the Horseman's Word.

The lore stretches back through infinity to the dark centuries when the horse was worshipped. It was said that the Celtic goddess Epona often visited this world in the guise of a horse, so any horse could be her, or could be related to her. This gave power to even the bones of the animal and a horse skull placed in the gable of a house would act as a talisman against evil.

Horses played a large part in the lives of the ancient Celts. The Greek historian Pausanius mentioned their horsemanship, horsemen riding into battle with two spare mounts and two followers ready to replace a wounded man or an injured horse. The horses themselves could be beautifully decorated with ornate harness discs of bronze, or colourful face masks which were sometimes buried with their aristocratic owners. Indeed, carvings of sacred horses still exist, from the giant chalk animal in Uffington in England to the light and graceful horse which prances from the Pictish stone at Inverurie in Aberdeenshire. Aberdeenshire in north east Scotland is considered the home of the Horseman's Word.

But all this adoration did not always auger well for the horse; when a Celtic king was crowned he frequently was called upon to mate – symbolically – a white mare, then to bathe in the broth of the slaughtered beast. He also had to eat and drink the mare's flesh and blood. This interesting rite continued until at least the twelfth century in Ulster.

There is still a faint echo of this in the habit of spitting three times at the sight of a white horse, but folklore has altered the origin to a memory of the Crusader's mighty stallions.

Perhaps it was those same Crusaders who helped replace Epona with St Michael as the patron of the horse. The Celts, with their love of horses, easily transferred their devotion – at least on the surface, for many of their cult practices remained unaltered save for the name.

Throughout Scotland, where once there had been races in honour of the Celtic goddess, now there were races dedicated to the Christian saint. St Michael's Day was celebrated on the 29th September and on the previous night it was customary to steal a horse to ride on the Saint's day. To prevent this, all stables were barred and men watched their mounts very closely, while no doubt contemplating the theft of a neighbour's horse. As the Gaelic proverb said:

Theft of horse on the feast of Michael
Theft that never was condemned.

Tradition demanded that no stable should be stripped completely so that each man had some sort of mount for the races. In North Uist every family sacrificed a lamb on Saint Michael's Eve and a special bannock was baked for the St Michael's Day Feast. After this, a local priest, clad in white like the druids or *culdees* of old and riding a white horse, led the entire community in a circuit of St Michael's burial ground.

With husband and wife sharing the same horse, and the song of Michael the Victorious being sung against the backdrop of a full harvest and crashing waves, the island was ready for the main event.

Riding bareback, with ropes of bent grass for a bridle and sun-dried seaweed for a whip, the young men raced beside the Atlantic breakers. Young women also raced, bareback like the men, often competing with them on equal terms. Celtic women were a match for their menfolk many centuries before the feminist movement!

Evening brought the pipes, dancing, and the discreet retiral of young couples, the women with rather suggestive presents of carrots for their chosen men, who soon pushed all thoughts of horses firmly to the backs of their minds.

Of course, not every horse race had religious connections. The Borders in particular were well known for both impromptu race meetings and the organised affairs which developed at the annual Common Ridings. These celebrations still continue, with sometimes hundreds of horsemen and horsewomen trotting round the boundaries of each border town, fording rivers and rough riding on makeshift race courses.

These ridings are very egalitarian events, with people from all walks of life participating, which is exactly as it was in the dark days when Border 'reiving' or raiding was a way of life. In the fourteenth century the Frenchman Froissart wrote that the fighting Scots 'were all a-horseback ... the common people on little hackneys and geldings'. Small in stature perhaps, but these border hobblers were so sure-footed they could pick their way across the menacing bogs and wind-blasted hill country of the borderland with ease. Indeed they were considered so important that Scottish kings imported breeding stock from Hungary, Spain and Poland, and exported to the Auld Enemy, England.

Further north could be found the garron, from the Gaelic *gearron* or gelding. These Highland ponies were often grey and able to cross the rough mountain terrain. Their descendants were, and are still, used to carry the victims of deer-stalking expeditions.

The islands also have their own distinctive animals – the Shetland pony is well known perhaps, but the Eriskay pony less so, and consequently in danger of fatal decline.

Widespread throughout Scotland was the belief in the psychic abilities of the horse. While a stallion was protected against witchcraft, and conveyed the same protection to his rider, all horses were gifted, or perhaps cursed, with second sight. Horses were prone to shy when passing a haunted site and often refused to pass a place where there had been a murder. Given the violence of much of Scotland's past, this must have made riding a tedious business.

All of this was well known to the Horsemen of Scotland's farming community, and more was gradually revealed to the initiate once he had been given the Horseman's Word. He would learn the secrets which had been passed from mouth to mouth by generation after generation of Horsemen. He would learn the Four Rules of Horsemanship –

To Make Him Stand;
To Make Him Lie;
To Make Him Hip;
To Make Him Hie.

He would learn about the herbs which made a man acceptable to a horse, and the substances, like toad's blood or pig dung, which were repellent to the animal. But first he had to learn the Horseman's Word.

At midnight, when the fields of Buchan or the Mearns stretched into the blackness beyond, the loon was taken to meet the devil, the Auld Chiel. Reeling with the whisky he had drunk, he was led to the darkest part of the stable. There on a rough bench or an ancient saddle sat a horned, hairy brute. Trembling, the loon was forced to hold out his hand and the apparition – hopefully the senior Horsemen – proffered the cloven hoof of some deceased farm animal. The two paws met and only then was the loon taken aside and the Horseman's Word whispered into his ear.

Then he was a Horseman, with power over horses (and women too!), with a station unmatched among the farm workers, and farm owners. A five year learning process lay ahead, but he had passed the initial test and could sing the toast with the best of them.

> *Here's to the horse with four white feet,*
> *The chestnut tail and mane,*
> *A star on his face and a spot on his breast,*
> *And his father's name was Cain!*

But what was the Word? Well, that is known only to the initiated.

TWO

THE GREY WOLF GAPING

OF all the animals which have prowled the hills and forests of Scotland, none have struck more terror in the hearts of folk than the wolf. Even the name is ominous – 'wolf'. It sounds as evil as the image it portrays, an image enhanced by scores of books and films in which the central villain is the half man half beast werewolf.

To the people of old Scotland – as to the people of much of Europe – the threat of the wolf was very real indeed. Tales abound of wolves and wolf hunts, of women and men attacked by wolves, of the last wolf killed in certain areas.

There was the great hunt in Rannoch for instance, early in the eighteenth century, when a wolf was chased into the Blackwood, south of Loch Rannoch.

Even with hounds it was extremely difficult to pursue a wolf through dense Highland woodland, but experience had taught the hunters how to flush out their quarry. When the forest was fired, the wolf loped from the northern fringe and plunged into Loch Rannoch. But, rather than drown, the wolf swam the entire breadth of the loch and ran for Ben a' Chuailaich.

In those days the area held a larger population than today and the aroma of a cooking fire drifted to the wolf from the local mill. Unable to resist the smell of food, the wolf followed the scent, shouldered open the unlocked door and entered the building. A fire crackled in the centre of the floor, with an iron cauldron suspended above, but the wolf ignored this and padded round the room, to the corner where a baby mewed from his cradle. The long grey mouth probed the bedclothes, the jaws opened ... but before the teeth clamped shut on the infant the goodwife came into the room.

It was every mother's nightmare, but the instinct for protection was strong and the goodwife attacked the wolf with the potato masher she carried. Enraged mother against hungry wolf? No contest! Soon the animal lay still, sprawled dead on the floor. From that time on the mill was known as 'Millinwadie' – Mill of the Wolf.

This story contains many of the elements traditionally associated with wolves – a hunt, the burning of a forest to flush the animal out, a defenceless child and a lone woman. Women figure in much of Scotland's wolf lore, and only rarely as a helpless victim.

There was Lady Margaret Lyon, the wife of the third Lord Lovat. Bred in the Lowlands, she moved north when married and was annoyed to find her new Highland domain plagued by wolves. Rather than be intimidated, she took the offensive and cleansed the Aird, inland from the Beauly Firth, of the beasts. Apparently she was 'a bold woman, a great huntress; she would have travelled in our hills a-foot, and perhaps out wearied good footmen'. If the 'good footmen' in question were the nimble Highlanders, Lady Margaret must have been formidable indeed.

The wolves of Argyll also learned to fear bold women. There are at least two versions of the tale of the last wolf in Argyll, but in each case it was a woman named MacDiarmid who was walking from Braevallich to Inveraray when a wolf leapt upon her from the forest. Swathing her arm with a shawl, the very able Ms MacDiarmid fended off the slavering, snapping jaws; but the wolf was desperate and gripped her even tighter. It was only a matter of minutes before the teeth penetrated the shawl, so the woman thrust her hand into the mouth, grabbed the long pink tongue, and held on until the wolf choked to death.

A similar tale was current in the Cairngorms, when a lone woman was attacked by a massive wolf near Lochanhully. As usual the wolf came off second best, mainly because the woman was carrying an iron griddle which she wielded with deadly skill.

These were all cases of individual animals, but in earlier times the Caledonian Forest – which covered a huge swathe of Scotland – fairly teemed with wolves: so much so that certain islands were used as graveyards to ensure the dead were not dug up and eaten by wolves. Innishail on Loch Awe was used for this purpose, as was the tiny islet of St Munda in Glencoe's Loch Leven. At other times stone coffins were used, but there were occasions when wolves were allowed free play.

The Norsemen were one of the major threats to early Scotland and their dragon ships ranged from Shetland to Galloway, spreading their unique brand of pagan horror. 'The Orkneyinga Saga', one of the laconic Norse poems which turns killers into heroes and mass slaughter into glorious victory, speaks of the aftermath of a battle in Skye where

> *... I saw the grey wolf gaping*
> *O'er wounded corse of many a man.*

Wartime was a blessing to the scavenger.

To the ordinary people the wolf was a menace, primarily because it preyed on the cattle which constituted Scotland's chief wealth. However, to the aristocracy, wolf-hunting was a pleasurable activity.

Deerhounds – the tall, shaggy dogs of Celtic Scotland – were used, and various kings passed Acts to encourage the extermination of wolves. By the 1280s there were professional wolf-hunters and the reward paid for killing the animals fluctuated throughout the centuries, depending on the state of the economy and the strength of the individual king's desire to quell the menace.

An Act of James I demanded that his Lords should 'chase and seek the quhelpes of wolves and gar slay them and sall give to the man that slays the woolfe twa shillings'. In 1491 this increased to five shillings, but later dipped to sixpence, rising in at least one instance in Sutherland to over six pounds. This latter instance, in 1621, reveals just how much the animals were feared.

Scots kings must have had a very difficult job as each attempt to pacify the country and to improve the lot of the good folk of Scotland was hampered by quarrelsome nobles and the constant threat of invasion from the south. Time and time again a period of peace would bring a rise in prosperity, a literary renaissance, increase in trade and agriculture, only for yet another spasm of warfare to bring anarchy and violence to Scotland. And then the wolves thrived.

Up in the Highlands, remote from invasion but subject to many local difficulties, wolves ghosted through the land. To safeguard the lone traveller, merchants, holy men or people on pilgrimage, places of refuge were established. These were known as 'hospitals', or 'spittals'.

By the end of the sixteenth century it was obvious that something had to be done about the wolf menace. Another Act ordering their destruction was passed in 1577, but in 1586 wolves were noted as being numerous and more drastic action was taken. This was the time of the burning.

Great areas of forest were torched to snuff out the wolves: sometimes locally, as in the case of the Blackwood of Rannoch; and sometimes on a larger scale. Accounts tell of forestland twenty miles long being burned around Loch Sloy. This degree of destruction is staggering, particularly when we consider how we are constantly urged to be conservation minded, but the Highlanders of the time considered conservation to mean protecting their own livestock. Wolves were a serious threat.

In time, with hunting and burning and felling of timber, the wolf was rooted out of Scotland. Cameron of Locheil is given the honour of killing the 'Last Wolf' in Killiecrankie in 1680, but twenty years later a man called Polson dirked another 'Last Wolf' in Glen Loth in Sutherland. To make the encounter more interesting, he caught it by the tail as it entered a cave which contained both the wolf's cubs and Polson's son.

Even later, in 1743, yet another 'Last Wolf' was killed, this time by a stalker named MacQueen. This was near the River Findhorn, not too far from the present Highland Wildlife Park where such wild creatures may again be seen today. Rather ironic.

The wild wolf has now gone from Scotland, but it is not forgotten. There are Wolfcleuchs in the Borders and Wolf Crags in the Pentlands, while the Highlands have Lochmaddy, Craigmaddy and Ardmaddy, from the Gaelic *madadh*, meaning a wolf.

The Gaels also termed the animal 'MacTire' – 'earth's son' – and amassed a stack of lore. Werewolf belief was once rife, with a potion of poppies, beladonna and datura being used to enable the change from man to wolf; but, strangely enough, a wolf's tooth, worn on a string round the neck, was supposed to bring luck.

And today? Visit a zoo or wildlife park and watch for a few minutes as the shaggy beast lopes across the ground. Witness the strength and agility. But, if the malevolent, untamed eyes turn to meet yours, imagine an encounter with a pack of such brutes on a lonely Highland track – and shudder.

THREE

BRAN, DON AND THE GREEN DOG

GLEN Lyon – *Gleann Dubh nan Garbh Clach*, 'the Crooked Glen of the Stones' – is the longest glen in Scotland and, according to legend, the headquarters of the Fian. Who were the Fian? Nine thousand Gaelic heroes led by Fionn himself – they were fighting men, hunting men and with them came their hunting dogs.

Not far from the village of Cashlie in the glen is the *Bhacain*, the two foot high Dog Stake where the hunting dogs were tied. Two of these dogs deserve to be remembered: the Grey Hound which once terrorised Glen Mhor, pouncing on stray humans and ripping them apart; and Fionn's own dog, Bran. Yellow-pawed, green-backed, black-flanked and tethered with a chain of pure gold, Bran was the finest, fastest, fiercest hunting hound ever.

Over sixty yards from the *Bhacain* you will find the *Caisteal Cain Bhacain* – 'the Castle of the Dog Stake'. From the long crumbled parapet food was tossed to the dogs. A long throw, perhaps, but the Fian were heroes and so were their dogs; it was instant expulsion for any dog who did not catch his supper.

If all this was true, there would be every reason to think that Bran was the ancestor of the modern Scottish deerhound, but unfortunately it is purely a story. The Fian were Irish Gaels who never set foot in Scotland and the tales travelled with Gaelic immigrants in the sixth century. The true lore of the stone castles of Glen Lyon will never be known. Never mind – Scottish dogs have enough qualities of their own and do not need imported legends.

Those mysterious people, the Picts, seemed to have a real affinity with animals and there is a deerhound carved in stone at Ardross which proves the ancestry of the dog in Scotland as well as any story. Lop-eared, shaggy, tall as a man's chest, the deerhound was taken to within sight of its quarry and released to chase down, or course, the deer. As a sport it was less one-sided than stalking, because the deer knew the territory and was bred to the wilds.

As late as 1858 deerhounds were used in deer coursing in the Duke of Atholl's Glen Tilt, but this was an unconventional hunt with an unconventional hunter. Samuel Baker was an eccentric, destined to buy a Hungarian slave girl, take her with him to explore the Upper Nile and, eventually, to marry her. But that day in particular he was out hunting. Unarmed except for his foot-long knife, unaccompanied except for two deer hounds, Baker used the dogs to drive and hold the deer while he ran alongside and stabbed the animal to death – ' … in my opinion,' he stated, it was 'ten times better sport than shooting a stag at bay'.

In reality the gentle deerhound was a dog of all trades. As well as hunting red deer and roe deer, it was used for boar and badger, fox and otter, while there was also the Scottish greyhound or Ratche, which might have been related.

Dogs feature in many Scottish tales, either in pursuit or as watchdogs. Sometimes dogs were used by the dominant Campbell Clan to hunt down fugitive MacGregors. Sometimes they even rose to national prominence: for example, when Robert The Bruce was hunted by English bloodhounds until he stood at bay, defending a ford against vastly superior numbers until reinforced. And sometimes they were quite simply 'out of this world'.

At one time the Highlands were thronged with fairy dogs. They were not of the Baskerville variety – *ie* they did *not* attack – but if they followed someone and barked thrice, death soon followed. The only protection was to turn and stone the dog at the first bark.

All the Highlanders knew this, so when the old shepherd near Ruthven Castle called in his own collie and instead a green dog with red ears and bright gold eyes slunk in, he was entitled to feel ill at ease. Highland hospitality, however, demanded that he treat the dog well, so it was fed and allowed to lie beside the glowing peat fire. There was a moment's tension when the collie came in and brindled at the uncanny presence, but within a few minutes both dogs were lying side by side at the fire.

The green dog left next morning, stopping only to lick the shepherd's hand in

gratitude. Surprising as the incident was, the shepherd had no time to ponder for a Cairngorm winter closed in, bleak and hard and bitter with blizzards. It was even more bitter when the shepherd's collie hurt her paw and could no longer herd the sheep. The shepherd took her inside, put on a dry birch-leaf poultice and left her to recover, while he tramped into the driving snow to seek out his sheep.

This was hard work, using the long crook to locate those animals lost in the drifts, digging them out and taking them to safety. With no collie to help him, the shepherd began to tire, every step getting heavier. As he turned for home he knew he had left it too late. The blizzard increased and he felt the cold biting into him. When the green dog suddenly appeared from a snow drift and stepped behind him, the shepherd slumped, expecting the three fatal barks.

But they did not come. The green dog moved closer and, for the second time, licked the shepherd's hand. At once a new warmth spread over him, some of the numbness lifted. Then the green dog barked – but only once – and half a dozen fairy dogs came out of the storm and expertly gathered the sheep into a sheltered corrie. The shepherd was led home by the first green dog, which licked him again; but when he tried to pat it, there was nothing there.

Tales of fairy dogs – Gaelic *Cu sith* – were fairly common, but there were other superstitions which were even more widespread. In Orkney it was bad luck for a dog to walk in front of a funeral procession; worse luck for the dog, which was often killed by relations of the deceased who would otherwise be the sufferers.

A howling dog was a death omen anywhere in Scotland and a strange dog entering a house meant a new friendship was imminent, but to be followed by a stray dog was good luck as well.

Sometimes a lone dog might not have been a stray. The old time cattle drovers were accompanied south by their dogs – collies mainly but probably rougher bred than the pampered lassie types which grace the show rings today. They might have been kin to the alert black and white border collies which most shepherds use. While the drovers remained in the south, the dogs were left to go home alone.

There was no cruelty in this. On the southward journey the drover always asked for food for his dog when he came to an Inn, and the dog called in at the same places while walking back north. The innkeepers kept faith with the drovers, knowing that they would be paid next year.

A similarly shaggy dog story is the rise of the terrier. Bred to hunt vermin – as foxes and otters were long considered, and sometimes still are – the Scottish terriers were rough, tough and capable of taking on anything their own weight and much that was heavier. The long-haired terriers were saved from an enjoyable, if hard-working, obscurity by Queen Victoria, who adopted them as she adopted many things Scottish. Now they are often pictured, white-haired and perky, sweetly sitting on the front of a shortbread tin with a tartan ribbon around their sturdy necks.

But terriers by no means have a monopoly on courage. There was Wallace, for example, the Fire Dog, an ordinary pet who quite literally ran away to join the Glasgow Fire Brigade. From 1894 to 1902 Wallace lived in the watchroom of the Central Fire Station, accompanying the engine to the scene of the fire and barking in unison with the clanging warning bells. Contrary to myths spread at the time, he was neither fireproof nor did he wear the specially made boots. And he certainly did not haul people out of burning buildings. That sort of heroics he would have left to an old seadog like Don.

A Rosehearty dog who would bark in pure Buchan Doric, Don was alert that October morning in 1904 when the German vessel 'Maria' was driven onto the rocks. There were eight coastguards at Rosehearty and all were present, as were a large percentage of the population. They stood on the shore and watched as rocket after rescue rocket failed to carry their line to 'Maria'.

The only hope was the banker's dog 'Don'. Rope in mouth, the black retriever jumped into the thundering surf. He struggled on, but the waves were too rough and he was forced back. Again he tried, and again he was beaten, but he persisted, returning a third time. From the beach the crowd watched him alternatively appear and disappear as he swam closer to the 'Maria', until at last the crew lowered a grappling hook, snatched the line and made it fast to the mast.

Don returned ashore and one by one the crew were rescued, with the ship's boy first and the captain last. Don was presented with a silver collar and he is still remembered today in Rosehearty.

The old time MacBrayne ferry captains were also helped by dogs, for when they were steering close to shore in thick fog they sounded their horns and the sound set all the local dogs barking. By the sound and quantity and location of the barks, the skippers, locals all, knew the dogs and to which croft they belonged and could review their position.

And today? Farm dogs, guide dogs, police dogs, sniffer dogs – they will surely be a part of Scottish society for ever. If not, we could always set loose Bran, 'the finest, fastest, fiercest hunting hound ever'!

FOUR

A DROVE OF CATTLE

SCOTLAND has always been cursed by having a large part of her economy rely on a single industry, be it mining, weaving or shipbuilding. From the mid seventeenth to the early nineteenth century this industry was cattle. Cattle-raising, cattle-breeding, cattle-droving: there was some truth in the statement that Scotland was little more than a grazing field for England, the chief export market.

Cattle, of course, had been important to Scotland long before the seventeenth century. In pre-Christian times cattle were invaluable and Celtic tribes raided their neighbours herds both to obtain stock and as a way of proving the manhood of young warriors. As significant was the religious practice at Beltane.

Beltane was a ceremony held on 1st May, when the god Belines, possibly related to the Biblical Baal, was honoured. Twin fires of sacred wood were built and cattle were driven between them to be purified from evil and disease. No doubt there would be incantations chanted and perhaps even a human sacrifice.

The ritual altered with the advent of Christianity. Human sacrifice was frowned upon by the Church and instead a square was cut in the ground with a section of turf left in the centre. A fire was built and a special meal of eggs, oatmeal, butter and milk was ritually offered to the ground and such animals as preyed on domestic stock. Only then were the cattle driven to the shielings to the words of *An Saodachadh* – the Driving:

> *The protection of Odhran the dun be yours*
> *The protection of Brigit the nurse be yours*
> *The protection of Mary the Virgin be yours*
> *In marches and in rocky ground*
> *In marches and in rocky ground.*

So important were cattle in early Scotland that parcels of land were not calculated by size, but by the number of cattle which could feed there. An echo of this exists today in place names like Oxgangs – the area ploughable by a team of oxen – in Edinburgh.

Next to land a man's wealth was measured by the number of cattle he possessed and often fines and taxes were paid in living beef. As were dowries, which could lead to complications if the amount of cattle did not equal the expectation of the husband – or the bride.

Although the Christian monks banned human sacrifice, they compensated by making stock breeding into a fine art. Settling in the Borders with its gentle hills and open land, the Roman Catholic Church, brought in by Queen Margaret I and her son David I, made the area Scotland's cattle country.

Rich pasturage and fat cattle protected by holymen: this was a tempting target for the wild men of the hills and the age old custom of cattle-stealing revived in Scotland – if it had ever stopped. As early as 1175 Parliament passed an Act making it unlawful to buy stolen cattle, but reiving or raiding was a game which endeared itself to the Scottish character. There was an element of sport, an element of skill, an element of danger and an element of gain; perfect for the half civilised men of the border valleys, or the wild men from the deep glens of the Highlands.

Scotland's history is punctuated with cattle raids. All the clans were at it – the MacGregors and MacFarlanes, Glengarry MacDonalds, Stuarts, Sinclairs, Scotts and the Armstrongs of Liddesdale.

Some clans specialised in reiving, raiding with their colours flying and pipes blaring in the full light of day. Some moved more stealthily by night – after all, wasn't the moon referred to as 'MacFarlane's Lantern'? And what about the Border slogan – 'There'll be moonlight again' – a motto of the Scott clan later penned by Sir Walter Scott?

On the Borders, the first months of winter were favoured for reiving: 'The depe of Winter and most unquiet season is come upon us,' the English official Thomas Scrope (1567-1609) wrote of Scottish raids. Robert Carey, another border-based Englishman, agreed gloomily, stating 'for then are the nights longest, they're horses at hard meat, and will ride best, cattel strong, and will drive furthest'.

In the Borders they rode the superb, if shaggy, hobbler, striking hard and escaping fast 'through unfrequented byways and many intricate windings,' as Bishop Leslie put it.

Sometimes there were pursuits and ambushes, sometimes full scale battles. This happened in the southwest Highlands with the Clan Gregor the instigator, and ultimately the main sufferer. In 1603 the MacGregors organised a cattle raid on the Colquhouns of Luss, in the course of which some unfortunate Colquhouns were killed. Naturally unhappy, their widows travelled to King James VI to show him the bloodstained shirts of their late husbands, augmented by others which had been spattered with the blood of a slaughtered sheep. When all this gore was shown to James, who was distinctly nervous when confronted with blood, he gave permission for the Colquhouns, or anyone else for that matter, to set upon the MacGregors with fire and sword.

Egged on by the Campbells, the MacGregors attacked again, bringing four hundred broadswords to Glen Fruin, defeating the Colquhouns in battle and escaping with some 600 cattle.

This raid resulted in the outlawing of the Clan Gregor. The name was banned, the gathering together of more than four ex-MacGregors was banned, the carrying of arms was banned, the very baptism of children was banned and it became legal, in fact it was encouraged, to kill any MacGregor. The cattle-raid was the excuse; the real reason was the land hunger of the Campbells. Cattle and politics frequently came together in old Scotland.

With all this activity it was not surprising that there were many superstitions concerning cattle. Cattle were vulnerable to witches and fairies, for instance, for both could steal milk from cows or transport milk from a cow owned by an enemy to one owned by a friend. Fairies were never seen doing this, for first they made themselves invisible, but the cattle owner could protect their animal by various methods.

Firstly there was elf shot, tiny flint arrow heads which are occasionally found in the earth. Worn by the farmer, these protected his animal against fairies and also against some diseases. If illness did strike, it was common to bury alive the first afflicted beast to protect the rest.

Birth too had its rituals, with cow dung spread over the mouth of a newborn calf to prevent the fairies from stealing the milk. And if a calf was stillborn, it was buried at the entrance of the barn and a prayer said to protect the remainder.

Witchcraft was a constant fear and rowan twigs or honeysuckle were hung in the byre on 2nd May, with red thread tied round the horns of the cattle to protect the milk. Pearlwort placed in the hoof of a mating bull – not an easy thing to do – would guard the future calf from witchcraft. Sometimes, particularly in the Western Isles, the blessing of Saint Columba was invoked in his role as the patron saint of cattle:

May the shepherd of St Columba
Be about your feet,
and may you come home safely.

Even so, the milk of a brown cow was considered better than a black or white animal, and the milkmaid still had to wash her hands after milking or the cow would run dry. After all this, the animal had to be tethered with rope made of horse hair to fend off witches.

Even when the cattle were driven to the summer pasture, the hind let a couple lag behind him, for the Evil Eye could only strike if all the beasts were to his front.

In Breadalbane the cattle knelt down on midnight on Christmas Eve, and if one of the Breadalbane family was about to die a bull would bellow and ascend the hillside. As it crested the rise, death occurred. Bulls signalled death in another way too – if a bull's head was brought into a feast it signalled a murder. The best known example of this is the murder of the young Earl of Douglas in Edinburgh Castle in 1440. Douglas was invited to the Castle by the king, assured of safe conduct. But at the feast a black bull's head was brought to the table – an old Scottish death warning. Douglas and his men were stabbed to death, resulting in a civil war – Douglas versus the king. The Royal army won – only just. If the king had lost, the Scots might have had a Douglas on the throne rather than a Stuart – with interesting consequences.

If the cattle survived the attention of reivers, fairies and witches, and still remained disease-free, the excess stock was driven south to the great trysts at Crieff or Falkirk or to the scores of local markets. There some were bought by local merchants and others were driven down to England.

The animals walked on recognised drove roads or over trackless hills, avoiding made roads with their toll gates and bridges which panicked the cattle. They forded rivers or used ferries in which the cattle were tethered nose first to rings in the gunwale. If they had to use hard roads they were roughly shod, and if any were injured the hirsute, honest drovers doctored them with Anchorage tar.

The trade continued for centuries until the drove roads became part of the landscape, until Marshall Wade followed their line for his military roads, until the Scots turned to sheep-breeding and deer-stalking for a new generation of Highland landlords.

However, in 1704 the export of cattle was still so important to Scotland that the English threatened to cease importing unless the Scottish parliament agreed to Ann rather than another James on the throne. So cattle played a very significant part in the Jacobite troubles.

Between reivers, witches and drovers, cattle have made a lasting impact on Scotland. Not bad for a simple, soft-eyed creature.

It is still possible to recapture some of the atmosphere of the old drover days. Visit one of the bare Border hillsides on a bleak autumn evening, with the wind flattening the heather. Faintly in the distance you might be able to imagine the drumming hooves and lowing of an approaching herd. Peaceful drovers or lance-wielding Armstrongs? Better not stay around to find out – keep it in the past and walk on … just in case.

FIVE

CONDEMNED TO WANDER THE SEA

THEY can be seen on most coasts of Scotland and always attract attention. Children love them, fishermen dislike them and tourist board photographers exploit them. In the past they have been hunted for their skins or severely left alone, gawped at, admired or reviled, but seldom viewed with total indifference. Seals are like that, with their incredible agility in the water and their habit of lounging in the waves to return the watcher's scrutiny with soulful eyes.

It is no wonder that legends grew up around these creatures. There were seals, or 'selkies', in the north and west coasts, but there were also sealmen and sealwomen. The former were quite simply that – seals; the latter a different species altogether, for the sealfolk could metamorphose into human beings.

According to naturalists there are two types of seals in Scottish waters. There is the common or round-headed seal and the larger grey or Atlantic seal which is also known as the dog seal as it has a long, dog-like muzzle. Only the dog seals could be seal-folk, and they only turned into humans on certain days, usually on Midsummer Eve, or 'Johnsmas' as it was known in the north. Other tales tell of metamorphism occurring every ninth night, or on the spring tide. Strangely, however, there is no indication of any fear of these 'were'-seals, possibly because they looked such gentle creatures.

In place of fear there was sympathy, for the sealfolk had once been human. However, they had transgressed in some way and had been ordered to roam the seas until Judgement Day, except for the odd night off. At these times they could be found on a lonely skerry with their sealskin coverings tossed aside as they danced away the short hours until dawn. Sometimes passing mariners witnessed them, the white bodies highlighted against the dark rock and the surging, unquiet sea.

That was one sure way of identifying sealfolk: they were always handsome, with faultless bodies, and although they had been compelled to wander the sea they were still sad to leave it for any length of time. Indeed, they were considered so beautiful that ordinary mortals fell in love with them after a single glance. There are many stories of this happening, one of which comes from Loch Duich.

Three brothers were fishing in the loch one midsummer when they saw a dozen seals glide ashore and flounder up a quiet beach. The seals looked around, but the brothers were in deep shadow and could not be seen. So off came the sealskins and the seals were transformed into humans – men and maidens. When moonlight glimmered on the beach, the three brothers gasped at the sheer loveliness of the seal maidens and decided to creep closer.

Only when it was time to return to sea did the three youngest and most beautiful of the seal maidens miss their sealskins. The brothers had stolen them, which meant they now had total power over the rightful owner. As the remainder of the sealfolk slipped into the waves they threw sorrowful glances at the three wailing maidens, but with dawn fast approaching there was nothing they could do. Two of the brothers quickly hustled their prisoners away, but the youngest was kind hearted and handed back his sealskin to a weeping maiden.

The youngest and prettiest seal maiden took her skin and escaped into the water. As she reached the edge of the loch she looked back, smiled her thanks and swam out to sea. Laughing at the softness of their kin, the other brothers married their maidens and hid the sealskins.

When midsummer came again the seals returned to Loch Duich and the youngest brother sat on a rock and watched his seal love capering with the rest. She saw him there, lonely and sad, and remembering his kindness found herself first liking, then loving him in return. They met again and her father, the leader of the sealfolk, agreed that they should marry. They lived happily for many years.

There was no such joy for the other brothers. The wife of one found her skin and fled back to sea. This frightened the second brother so much that he set fire to his sealskin.

His wife saw the flames, tried to douse them, but was tragically killed in the fire.

Stories like this were widespread along the coasts and islands of Scotland, although mainly in those regions which were once influenced by the Norse culture. One Norse legend states that it was unlucky to kill or hurt a seal in case it was an emissary of the King of Lochlann (the old name for Norway).

In Gaelic the seal is called *ron* and the tiny island of North Rona, most northerly of all the Hebrides, might mean Seal Island. Of course, it might just as easily take its name from St Ronan who sailed here on his *currach* or coracle to find peace from the prattling women of Lewis.

The MacCodrums in particular would never hurt a seal, for they were known as Clan MacCodrum of the seals. A North Uist clan, some had been enchanted so they became seals by day and human at night, although all the time they kept their human souls.

In most tales it is the seal maiden who is forced to live ashore by the theft of her skin, but there were times when a human woman desired a sealman as lover. To obtain one, the woman had to shed seven teardrops into the sea when the tide was full, and a sealman would appear. They would make love and nearly always the union was fruitful.

One unlucky woman from Yell in Shetland met a sealman face to face while innocently gathering shellfish. At least that was the excuse she gave nine months later when she produced a bonny bouncing baby. Superstition could be very convenient sometimes.

It was easy to recognise the progeny of such sweet encounters, for they had webbed fingers and toes and thick horn skin, or sometimes scales, on the soles of their feet and the palms of their hands. The Mackays of Borgie in Sutherland were said to be like this and were known as the 'descendants of the seal'. It is also interesting that as recently as the nineteenth century there were people in North East Scotland with webbed toes who were thought to be lucky – because, no matter what happened, they could never drown.

Sometimes sealmen and humans could help one another. Herman Perk was a seal hunter from Papa Stour in Shetland. One day he was on the Vee Skerries when a huge wave threw him into the sea. He struggled bravely but was near to drowning when a seal nudged him above the waves and dragged him ashore on Papa Stour. To thank his rescuer Perk found the skin of the animal's sealmaiden wife and returned it to her as she sat naked and weeping on the beach. She dressed quickly, for it must have been embarrassing with a hulking Shetland hunter watching – then the sealmaiden slipped back into the sea and swam to her husband.

Other seal stories are true, rather than legend, but just as warming, like the saga of the young dog seal which was caught by fishermen off the Treshnish Isles. The fishermen brought it back to Mull and treated it as a pet until it became too pampered to fish and took to eating hens instead.

Naturally the fishermen were not too happy at this and they returned the seal to the Treshnishs, expecting it to revert to its natural habits. Following the herring round the coasts, it was weeks before they were back in Mull, and there in the bracken was their pet seal, waiting for them. It seems that there is more similarity to the dog seal and the dog than just the name.

SIX

BIRDS
OF
ODIN

EVEN today there is something sinister about a lone crow, and the rustle of many wings as a flock of rooks return home in the early dusk can be faintly disturbing. There is no real wonder in this, for these birds are large and black and powerful enough to be a real danger to a new born lamb, or to a tiny baby.

But perhaps there is something deeper in our aversion, something which goes back to the days when the raven was symbolic of a pagan god; and the hooded crow, the maligned 'hoodie', might be the terrifying *Cailleach* herself.

Like so many gods in the Celtic pantheon, the *Cailleach* was a creature best avoided. She dwelt mainly in the Celtic Otherworld, beneath the ground or beyond the western ocean, but was known to visit our world disguised as a hooded crow. When she did so death and destruction followed in her wake. Celtic goddesses were as feared as Celtic gods, just as Celtic women were as powerful as Celtic men. Perhaps this ability to grant equality shows a civilisation more advanced than its contemporaries, but more likely it is based, at least partly, on fear: the fear of the dominant mother/wife as shown by the effigy of *Sheela-na-gig* – a representation of the Celtic god of creation and destruction – in places like the Church of St Mary and St David in Kilpeck, England.

Be that as it may, until recently gamekeepers shot the hoodie on sight and possibly they still do. But that is more to do with game management than terror of ancient gods.

There are people today who still think it unlucky to see a single crow and would dread to hear its harsh caw coming from the left, for that is a sure sign of bad luck. The crow seems to carry luck on its wings, much as the magpie does, for if a crow scrapes and flutters against a window it means death for someone, and four crows flying together over a house will bring suffering to the occupants.

However, there is a glimmer of silver on the cloud of black plumage, for if two fly above a house, it's time to buy nappies and prepare for nights of broken sleep – a birth or a wedding is forecast.

It was also bad luck for a crow to perch on the mast of a boat and thus bring the shadow of disaster to the voyage.

An interesting belief comes from Shetland. On the morning of Candlemas – 2nd February – the young unmarried women used to follow the first crow they saw in the hope that it would lead them to their destined husband. Sometimes the crow brought them to the house in which they would live; sometimes it flew to the kirkyard. In the latter case the girl knew she would never wed.

There was nothing romantic in the Border conception of the crow, as the ballad of 'The Twa Corbies' tellingly reveals. This is a tight little picture of a man deserted by his woman, his hawk and his dog – probably all the things he most cared for in life – as seen by a chillingly callous pair of corbies, or crows. As an illustration of the crows as the harbinger of evil it could hardly be bettered:

> *Ye'll sit on his white hause bane*
> *And I'll pick out his bonny blue een:*
> *Wi' ae lock o' his gowden hair,*
> *We'll theek our nest when it grows bare.*

The idea of these great black birds being able to talk stretches back, like so much, to the Norse. The Raven was known as the 'Bird of Odin' and so was honoured by the Vikings. To the Gaels, inveterate enemies of the Norse, these birds foretold death. This is not surprising when the Norse god Odin was known as Hrafna-god, or 'God of the Raven', and he had two ravens who were something more than pets. These two, Hugin and Munin, spent the daylight hours spying on the people below so they could tell Odin what they had seen.

With such a background it is not surprising that the raven was used on a flag. In about the ninth century, Norse power in Scotland was centred in Orkney and stretched from Muckle Flugga at the tip of Shetland to Islay and was still expanding on the mainland. Although the sparsely populated islands and far north had been claimed, the Norse found considerable difficulty penetrating south east of the Great Glen, where the Picts stood firm.

Sigurd, Earl of Orkney, was confronted by the *Mormaer* (the Pictish equivalent of an earl) of Moray – a man named Finnleik. No one could doubt the courage of the Norse, but the Picts were a formidable foe who had already defeated an Anglo-Saxon invasion and held their own with the Scots, so Sigurd ran for help to his mother – hardly the act expected of a Viking warrior. Sigurd's mother perhaps thought this also and said, somewhat scornfully, that if she had suspected that her son wanted to live forever she would have raised him in her wool basket. Heartened by her guidance nonetheless, Sigurd sallied forth to do battle, but not before his mother gave him a gift to prove her maternal affection.

This was the famous Raven Banner of Orkney. The raven apparently raised his wings when Orkney was triumphant, but drooped if the enemy won. On this occasion the raven could be rampant, for Sigurd won his battle. (Perhaps his mother fought his battles for him!)

Ravens retained their power to awe long after the Norse had been defeated and become part of the living blood of Scotland. There was a belief, held from Shetland to the furthest of the Outer Isles and inland at least as far as the Cairngorms, that the raven could produce a magic pebble. This stone was known as the 'Raven Pebble' in the mainland, the 'Victory Stone' or 'Seringsten' in Shetland and the *Clach Dotaig* – stone of virtue – on St Kilda.

In each case it took great effort to obtain. A raven's nest had to be robbed of its eggs, which were boiled and returned. Being an intelligent bird, the raven would realise that something was wrong and so it flew away to seek the Raven Pebble. This was a small, transparent stone which, according to the mainland legend, the bird rubbed against the eggs to re-fertilise them. In the mainland version, a man who held this stone and put it inside his mouth would become invisible, but only if he intended to do good. If he used the power of the stone for anything evil he would suffer some horrible calamity.

In the Shetland Isles the stone had the effect of bringing prosperity and good fortune, while saving its owner from the attentions of the Trolls – evil dwarf-like creatures of Norse mythological origin – which must have been a great relief. The St Kilda version also brought good luck to the virtuous.

Some of the raven lore actually may be older than the Vikings – for instance, there was the belief that it was unlucky to kill a raven because it held the soul of King Arthur. This idea was never particularly widespread in Scotland, perhaps belonging to the Brythonic Celts of Wales, Cumbria and Strathclyde and dying out with the take-over of the south west of Scotland during the early mediaeval period.

The unfortunate raven was condemned to be black and to exist on a diet of carrion because of an ancient ancestor sent out by Noah to check on the receding Flood. It did not return to the Ark and was thereafter condemned, but as this is hardly the action of a forgiving God, little credence should be given to the story.

Eating the eggs of a raven had the effect of turning the eater's skin black, which could be interesting, but at least in the Highlands it was good luck to hear the croak of a lone raven.

Overall, the crow, raven and associated rook are unchancy birds to have around, with a grim history. There was even a raven witch in Caithness, one *Fitheach* – which means 'raven who had the ability to change herself into a hare'. Unfortunately for her, she ran into a snare while out a-haring and was found next morning as herself ... dead – which is how most farmers would like to see the local crows and rooks. They remain as unpopular as ever.

SEVEN

FRIENDS OF THE LORD

A WESTERLY wind slammed in from the Atlantic with enough bite to make the man gasp. He ran on, stumbling over the machair, glancing over his shoulder at his pursuers. The white robe he wore flapped at his knees so he lifted it and ran on.

It was dull, dreich beneath low grey skies. The sea to his left crashed onto endless damp sand. He was not used to such a climate, but this was still part of his father's Kingdom, still part of his heritage and he belonged. Also, there was a strange beauty here, not the hard edged clarity of his birthplace but a subtle merging of colour and atmosphere, a harmony of sound and vision and scent which was gradually penetrating his soul. And he knew all about souls.

Armour clattered behind him, the thud of military footwear on sand, and there were shouts in Latin, harsh against the whistling birdcall all around. The man rounded a headland, hoping for somewhere to hide – but there was nowhere. Machair and beaches, moorland spattered with rippling lochans, and beyond that the sea and another, higher, island. He glanced back once more and heard the Latin, bowed his head and said a short prayer.

As if in answer a pair of birds landed smoothly at his side. They were all black with straight red beaks and he could understand their calls. Lying in a slight hollow where the beach met the machair, the man heard the birds whistling to each other, felt the damp weight of seaweed as it was piled on top of him. There was the vibration of footsteps and he ducked his head, smelled the tang of brine and heard again the Latin.

Confused questions, the perplexed anger of frustration and more footsteps, receding, and then only the surge of the sea and the sweet whistle of the birds. The man waited for a while, and then a bit longer, and only then he emerged, pushing the sand-smeared seaweed from his body. Of the searchers there was no sign, but the two birds circled still, calling to each other.

The man raised both arms until they extended at right angles from his body; and as he looked upward at the birds an aureola, a glorifying halo, emanated from his head. There was power here and the two birds were drawn down to land.

'I am the Christ!' the Man stated. 'From this day you and your descendants will be blessed; you will wear the cross on your breast and wings and you will continue your good deeds by warning seafarers of bad weather by calling out to them!'

There is no documentary data to support this story, but the circumstantial evidence is

so overpowering that it could well be true.
Firstly there is the appearance of the birds –
they still fly the length and breadth of
Scotland, and further afield, bearing the cross
of Christ across their body. This is the oyster-
catcher, no longer all-over black.

Secondly there is the warning: the oyster-
catcher continues to warn seamen by calling
'bi glic! bi glic!' when there is a storm
approaching. *Bi glic* is, of course, 'be careful'
in Gaelic, the tongue spoken by Adam and
Eve in Eden.

And thirdly there is the hard fact that
nowhere in the Bible does it state that Christ
was captured in the Western Isles of Scotland.
Therefore He apparently escaped.

Because of their assistance to Christ, the
oystercatchers were named *Gille Brighde* by
the Gaels: the 'guide' or 'servant of Bride'.
This was St Bride, the foster mother of Christ,
who baptised Him by touching his brow with
three drops of spring water on the morning
of His birth. In Gaelic society a fostermother,
like a fosterfather or brother, was every bit as
important as a natural parent, and in reality
Bride fostering Christ was symbolic of the
Gaelic people fostering Christianity, making
it their own.

St Bride was the Christian version of the
Celtic goddess Brigit, who was the daughter
of the god Dagda – *Deagh Dia*, the 'Good
God' – which in itself might have some
significance. St Bride's Day,
or the Feast of St Brigit, was
held on 1st February. The
Christian celebration of

Candlemas, remember, is on 2nd February.

Before the advent of Christianity, 1st February was the Celtic feast of Imbolg, one of the major celebrations of the year and possibly the start of the lambing season. Brigit, or Bride, was honoured throughout the Celtic world and there are many churches which carry her name. One such church was in Douglasdale in Lanarkshire (Douglas is *dhu glas*, 'black water', in Gaelic) and none other than Sir James of Douglas, the Good Sir James, was said to retain St Bride as his personal saint. This was the same Douglas who supported Bruce in his defence of Scottish independence, so the best of the Celtic gods joined forces with a Christian king to fight off an extremely nasty takeover bid. No doubt, then, that the Gille Brighdes would have called their warning at the approaching storm of war.

In that same eventful trip to the Western Isles, Christ was seen by another band of enemies. Who His enemies were is not specified, but they might well have been Roman soldiers; after all, Pontius Pilate was, according to some accounts, born in Perthshire. Anyway, this time Christ took refuge in a South Uist barn, where the farmer hid Him under a pile of oats. It was only a small pile and it left parts of Christ sticking out, so the farmer dashed to a neighbour for more oats, leaving Christ alone. Or not quite alone ... for the ducks and hens piled into this unattended free feed.

As Christ lay there and the searching soldiers tramped outside, the hens scattered the oats, revealing more of the fugitive – but the ducks were more pernickety and pecked at the loose grain first. Once the Romans had left, Christ rose from his concealment and granted the ducks three blessings: the blessing of life above water, the blessing of life on water, and the blessing of life under water. On the other hand, the power of flight was taken from the hens, who also became afraid of wind, hail, rain and snow.

Even on the east coast ducks were believed to have special powers, for the farmers of Angus used to suspend a dead duck head down to chase evil from the house, while if duck eggs were brought into a house at night they would not hatch.

The belief that the robin received its red breast as it tried to pull a thorn from Christ's head, so becoming stained with Holy blood, is not unique to Scotland; nor is the story of the robin being scorched by the fires of Hell as it brought water to the souls suffering there.

What *is* unique is the story of St Servanus of Culross who let his pet robin perch on his shoulder. A gang of ruffians killed the bird, which upset the old saint, but help was at hand in the person of St Kentigern, Glasgow's own saint, who brought the robin back to life. So instead of standing on the shoulders of a saint, the robin took pride of place in the coat of arms of Glasgow: what better home could a robin have?

The Gille Brighde, of course, is at home on any Scottish coast, and is so good at storm forecasting that the people of St Kilda know what weather is approaching at any given time. But it was off Skye that they again proved their worth.

Three small children were playing beside Loch Eishort one summer day when the heat overcame them and they crawled into one of the beached boats and fell asleep. As they slept the tide came in and their boat drifted out to sea.

The children awoke to the whine of a rising wind and the warning call of the Gille Brighde. Looking around, they realised that they had been carried out of Loch Eishort, past Strathaird Point and were in the Cuillin Sound, heading for the Little Minch. Island bred, they tried to row ashore, but they were too small and the heavy oars slipped from their fingers.

Above them the birds were circling, calling 'bi glic! bi glic!' and the children waved to them, shouting for help. The oystercatchers heard and swooped back to Skye and the township of Kilbride, 'church of Bride', in Strath, beneath the slope of Beinn na Caillich.

St Bride was at home. She listened to the call of her servants and let them guide her to the frightened children. Walking barefoot over the waves with her arms full of bog cotton to cushion the hard wood of the boat, she towed it back to Loch Eishort and safety.

And above circled the Gille Brighde, calling, guiding, and the cross was glowing white on the dark feathers.

EIGHT

CREATURES OF THE HILLSIDE

THEY had come that morning from Pitlochry and now an early afternoon sun was cleansing the mist from the hill flanks. There was little sound, save for the rasping of breath, the hollow thud of heavy boots and the chink and rustle of equipment. The mist thinned rapidly now, revealing more of the spectacular scenery, and the bearded man turned and grinned to his companion.

'Nearly there!'

She nodded, forced a smile, then pointed abruptly upward. 'Look! What's that?'

It was a face, white-bearded, ferociously horned, peering down at them from the summit of Ben Vrackie. Not a pleasant face with its yellow eyes and long jaw. Then both climbers laughed as they realised what it was.

'A goat! It's a wild goat!'

Feral goats are native to Scotland and are still frequently seen in the hills, both in the Highlands and in the Southern Uplands, although their presence was not always welcomed. This was due in part to their destructive habits, particularly in the forests where they eat tree bark and branches. The foresters of old Scotland took drastic action, either hanging the offending goat – or any goat they could catch – by the horns from a tree, or killing it outright and leaving the creatures bowels as a grim warning.

There was also the possibility that what appeared to be a goat might in reality be a *Uraisg* (or *Uruisg*) – a monstrous brute, half man, half goat, which infested various places in the Highlands. Such a creature lived in the corrie of Coire-nan-Uraisg in the Cuillin hills in Skye and it was reported to have long hair, long teeth and long claws. It is also a long time since the Uraisg was last seen.

A third, and even worse, possibility was meeting Lucifer in goat form. With cloven hooves and yellow eyes, the Scottish 'Auld Hornie' was a clever wee devil and up to all the tricks as he waited beside a burn for his victim. Definitely one to avoid, although it is said that novice Freemasons and witches were often seen riding 'widdershins', the wrong way round, on a billy goat. Which is perhaps a further reason for the animal's apparent unpopularity.

This unpopularity is misleading, for domesticated goats were extensively farmed in Scotland, so much so that they probably outnumbered both cattle and sheep.

Rob Roy MacGregor for instance, famous outlaw and redcoat baiter, possessed about two dozen goats but only twelve cattle and twelve sheep. In the closing decades of the seventeenth century, the Highlands were sending 100,000 goat and kid skins a year to London, which proves both their quantity and their economic value.

However, not all the animals were necessarily Highland bred. Huge herds of Lowland goats were taken north to be sold in a form of reverse cattle drove, with the luckier, or more skilled, drover selling his stock before he penetrated too deeply into dangerous clan territory. It was not unknown for predatory robber chiefs to relieve the Lowlander of the burden of unsold stock.

Many of these travelling goats would escape and form the nucleus of the wild herds which can be seen today and which have played their part in Scottish history.

During the black years, when the English strived to conquer Scotland and every glen and Border dale was a potential centre for resistance, King Robert The Bruce was at a low ebb. Defeated by treachery at Methven, ambushed by the MacDougalls at Dalrigh, his army scattered, he lay in a cave at Inversnaid – MacGregor country. Outside were his enemies, English and Scots who supported his royal rival Comyn, searching for him. They were bound to find the cave soon, so Bruce gripped his sword and waited. Footsteps outside, a body blocking the sunlight and Bruce rose ... to see a wild goat. Ignoring him completely, the goat lay across the entrance of the cave, joined by another ... and another.

Quiet voices outside, a muttered comment about their being no king where there were goats, and the searchers moved on. When it was safe Bruce emerged. As the goats had saved his life, he ordered that they too be kept safe, declaring the entire area a goat sanctuary.

The people of the Highlands had many uses for goats. As well as the obvious, food and drink, goats milk was – and is – said to be good for health and beauty. A craze for whey-drinking swept Scotland in the eighteenth century, with people flocking to various places which specialised in that particular pastime. In a way it complemented the mineral water cult which saw mock-Grecian temples adorn health-giving spa wells.

Goats were also used to drive off evil, being brought near sick people to take away the disease, or forcing the evil fairies from border hills. The fairy belief lasted until comparatively modern times, with the grandfather of James Hogg – 'Jamie Hogg the Poeter' – regularly speaking with them.

Another widespread story claimed that goats killed adders by using both horns and hooves. For this reason alone goats would be prized, for adders had the reputation of being prolific sheep killers. If the sheep was merely injured there was a chance of recovery, provided the shepherd could lay hands on a 'snakestone'. One of the many Scottish stones with magic properties, this was a small stone pierced with a hole, through which snakes were said to slither to cast their old skin. If this was dipped in hot water, which was then used to wash the bitten part of the sheep, a cure was nearly certain.

The shepherd without a snakestone had more choices – he could kill the adder, decapitate it and rub the head against the bite, or dry the head and use it as a snake-stone.

Or he could invest in some goats, onions or ash trees. Although the latter was perhaps not a practical proposition in the hill country, it was believed that a branch of ash or a raw onion drove off snakes in the same manner as garlic kept away vampires. Unfortunately, these articles would also chase off the rare white adder which, if seen, was a symbol of good luck.

The best day to see this snake, or any other, was St Brides Day when the snakes appeared from their family home. To ensure a snakebite-free year, it was customary to greet the emerging reptiles with a cheery wee ditty:

Early on Bride's morn,
The serpent shall come from the hole
I will not molest the serpent
Nor will the serpent molest me.

There are other versions, but the idea is always the same.

Throughout Scotland, as in many other countries, there are tales of giant, snake-like creatures. Of these the two best known are the Linton Worm from the Borders and the Stoor Worm from the Northern Isles. The Linton Worm was a nasty brute which lived in a tunnel in Linton Hill, coming out twice a day to eat. Everything and anything disappeared into its cavernous, poison-fanged mouth and the locals could do nothing against it, for weapons bounced from its tough scales.

Eventually a local knight, John Sommerville, killed the worm by thrusting a burning peat down its throat. The worm's writhings brought its own tunnel crashing down so it was crushed to death.

The Stoor Worm was even worse, a direct descendant of the Norse World Serpent whose evil body coiled round the entire globe. Every Saturday the Stoor Worm ate seven maidens, presumably one for every day of the week. Eventually this too was killed when a farm boy rowed out to do battle, was predictably swallowed and burned the worm's liver with a flaming peat. (Maybe the crofters of the north have ulterior reasons for maintaining their peat stacks.)

A snake from the Northern Isles would have to be seaborne, for there are no land snakes in Orkney or Shetland, which fact determined the political position of Stroma. This is a small island in the Pentland Firth, guarded by whirlpools, tide races and sudden fogs. In the past it has been the home of smugglers and superb seamen, but once it was the centre of a dispute between the Earl of Caithness and the Earl of Orkney.

Both wanted Stroma, both claimed the island as part of their earldom. To ascertain to whom Stroma belonged, adders were brought to the island and set free: if they survived, Stroma was obviously part of Caithness, which had reptiles; but if they died, Stroma was one of the Orkney Islands, which were snake-free.

The snakes lived and Stroma became the

only island in Caithness – a judgement worthy of Solomon. Of course, if the Earl of Orkney had thought things out, he could have sneaked some goats onto the island – but perhaps he was too fair-minded for that.

NINE

LORE OF THE WATER

NOWHERE in Scotland is far from water. We have three seas – the North, the Atlantic and the Irish – we have lochs as legendary as Leven, Lomond and Ness, we have famous rivers like the Tweed, Clyde and Spey. It has also been rumoured that rain has been known to fall.

So it should not be surprising that a great deal of Scotland's folklore centres on the creatures which live in and around water: the birds, fish and mammals which were daily seen and which played a major part in people's lives. Scottish rivers were once so crowded with salmon that even the lowly apprentices were glutted with them, demanding that they were not served salmon more than thrice a week. This seems an exaggeration, but there are too many salmon stories to totally discount the legend.

There was the Laird of Kinchurdy, for instance, who kept a net in one of the many pools of the Spey. When a salmon blundered into the net, it jerked a rope which rang a bell and alerted the cook. Fresh salmon daily, at no cost and little labour.

Being a Fraser, one of the Lords Lovat went one better. While hunting beside the River Beauly he lit a fire of sticks and placed a pot of water on top. As the water heated, one of the salmon which filled the river leapt out, straight into the pot.

And they did fill the rivers. Speaking of the Dulnain River, a fisherman said there were 'extraordinary much kipper [*ie*, salmon near to spawning] which are in abundance, that a gentleman thinks nothing to kill 160 in a night'. There was a slightly sour ending when it was noted that the 'gentlemen' avoided any fine for poaching, while the 'commonality' were not so lucky – if they were caught! Poaching is still second nature to many Scots.

Sometimes poaching required little effort, as on the River Shin at the end of the eighteenth century when large baskets were positioned beneath the Falls to catch those salmon which failed to make the leap. Possibly only the weakest or the most stupid fish were caught, for salmon in general had a reputation of possessing wisdom. This might refer to their uncanny sense of direction which enables them to return to spawn year after year, but it could be a throwback to the days of St Fingal, who ate the salmon whose meat held all the world's wisdom.

However, they were also rather sexist fish. A man had to be first to cross the Barvas River in Lewis every May-day, for if a woman crossed first the salmon would be offended and would not come that year.

Although there is so much salmon lore, which is surely a pointer to its importance, other fish were not ignored. If a fisherman caught a carp it was believed he could expect a year of prosperity, while in the northern isles a skate was welcomed as an aphrodisiac.

Herring, the 'silver darlings' and mainstay of the Scottish fishing fleet for much of last century, were very sensitive fish. When two fishermen drowned themselves in Loch Carron, the herring shoals fled out to sea and only returned when bonfires were built on the exact spot where the bodies were washed ashore.

To ensure that herring remained in their inshore fishing grounds, they had to be eaten from tail to head. If they were eaten head to tail the herring would turn *en masse* and swim for the open sea. Yet like so many other Scottish creatures, they had a medicinal quality and if rubbed on the bare feet they could cure a sore throat. Nautical acupuncture without the sharp pins.

When the fishermen were out hunting, they were always pleased to see a porpoise, which brought luck and also fended off any sharks. More than two was even better as full nets were guaranteed, but seamen kept a wary eye on them if they frolicked too hard – that meant heavy weather.

Occasionally the fishermen would haul up an eel, which was kept, for the skin when wrapped round the thigh prevented cramp. If worn round a sprain, the fat eased the pain and the pliable skin stretched with the swelling. Eels, of course, were often thought to grow from horse hairs dropped in the water, and if they came on land they would turn into snakes. That was a frightening thought. One conger eel caught in Scrabster harbour in Caithness weighed 45 lbs – a formidable weight for a snake.

However interesting the fish, it was the birds which really caught the imagination. Mysterious, gravity-defying, owning powers denied to mankind, birds are natural repositories of myth. One of the most nautical of all birds must be the storm or stormy petrel. The smallest of all web-footed birds at only eight inches long, and dark coloured with white round the tail and beneath the wings, the stormy petrel is known to follow ships in the Hebridean and northern seas.

To the old seamen a stormy petrel hovering above the ship was an ill omen, to be repelled by having a horseshoe fastened to the mast. The magic power of horses and of iron was well known, the combination of both made a horseshoe very potent against evil.

The stormy petrel was known in Gaelic as *gur-le-gug* which loosely translates as 'hatch by a cluck', because while hatching its eggs the petrel clucks to itself. This can be disconcerting if heard at night on one of the more remote islands of the west or north, which is exactly where it nests. More distressing, however, is the uncanny shriek of the manx shearwater which is something akin to the banshee – only worse.

For once, a bird's Lowland name is more evocative than the Gaelic. *Petrel* means 'little Peter' and comes from the petrel's habit of fluttering just above the sea with its legs pointing down and its feet touching the surface, like St Peter walking on water. Seamen often call them 'Mother Carey's Chickens', 'Mother Carey' being a nautical corruption of *Mater Cara,* the Blessed Virgin Mary.

More attractive in appearance is the puffin, whose multi-hued bill and bright red feet make it a firm favourite with children and photographers. This is a cheeky, stocky little bird, only one foot in height, which colonises various isolated islands. The puffin, or sea parrot to the east coast fishermen, has the endearing habit of guiding its young out to sea on their maiden flight.

In Gaelic the puffin was known as *Seamus Ruadh* – which can be charmingly translated as 'Red Jimmy' – for their big red feet; while up in Shetland they were known as 'Tammie Noorie'.

Most common of all seabirds are the gulls, from the fork-tailed tern or sea swallow, to the predatory great black backed gull which kills for fun. To the seamen of old, all seagulls were the unquiet souls of drowned mariners and as such should neither be hurt nor killed. The stormy petrel was included in this assessment, as was the albatross of the southern ocean. Perhaps this seems a long distance from Scottish folklore, but Scottish whalers roamed the cold waters of the south – hence the Edinburgh-based name Leith Harbour in South Georgia. And were the famous James Weddell and James Clark Ross, Antarctic explorers both, not Scots, with Scots seamen in their crew?

To these men the Albatross was not only a flying soul, but also a flying tobacco pouch. At least their webbed feet were. A poor reason for killing a fine bird.

The black headed gull, smallest and most common of the seagulls, has a story all of its own. *Stuirteags* in Gaelic, these birds nested far inland and it was the people of the Cairngorms who thought they carried the souls of caring people. These people did good all their lives and would qualify as angels once they extirpated the few sins they could not help but commit. The black face and head, gradually diminishing as autumn approaches, is a symbol of their fading sin; and as they were nearly pure in life, in death they are the messengers of the angels.

TEN

THE WITCH'S CAT

HOME of the wild MacNeils, whose pirate galleys once roved from Ireland to Ardnamurchan, Barra has long been famed as a repository of Scottish culture and folklore. One Barra lady was in the habit of leaving her home every night, much to the chagrin of her husband. One night, suspecting the worst, he waited until she had closed the door and followed her into the dusk. A soft wind swept in from the sea and there was silence, save for the shush of gentle breakers and the padding of his wife's footsteps on the moor.

Grim faced, the husband watched, expecting to see another man, but he gasped and crossed himself when his wife suddenly dropped onto all fours and changed into a shaggy black cat. Frozen to the spot, he could do nothing as another cat appeared, then another, until there were eight. They huddled together, dim shapes in the dimness of a Hebridean night, and their united screeching wails awoke the hills. A name was mentioned, the Devil was invoked, and the cats launched a sieve onto the wide Atlantic.

THE WITCH'S CAT

The concept of people changing into animals was not unknown in Scotland. Witches seemed to spend half their lives jumping from human to animal and back again. They usually took the form of a cat or a hare, sometimes a horse, and there is even a case of a witch changing into a whale off Skye. All the same, it must have been disconcerting for the husband to see his wife cavorting around a beach with her tail in the air. There was only one thing to do: the husband called upon the Holy Trinity and the sieve upturned, drowning its entire feline crew.

This might seem rather a drastic method of correcting an errant wife, but cats were a powerful force in Scotland, frequently feared and nearly always held in some awe. Here it was a white cat which personified evil while a black cat brought luck, particularly if a hand was smoothed gently down its back. Failing that, a black cat crossing from right to left – sunwise – was always a good omen, but that was about all cats had going for them.

Like some other animals, they could be used as a minor weather vane: a cat sitting with its back to the fire indicated frost to come, while a playful cat which ran round the room was a forecast of high winds – neither weather condition uncommon in Scotland. More significantly, a cat washing its ears brought rain, and as cats are clean animals, it rains frequently in Scotland. Blame the cat!

On the other hand, cats have a long history. When the Norse came to Scotland, they applied their own names to the landscape. The north west of the country became Sutherland, 'south land', which it was to them – but the north east was Katanes, the 'headland of the cat people'. This area is now known as Caithness, while the Gaelic name for the whole north was *Cataibh* – 'land of the cat people'.

At this period the Gaels had not reached the far north, Gaelic power centred around Argyll, and this area was purely Pictish and therefore enemy territory. The Duke of Sutherland, whose forebears were no friends to the Gael, is known as *Morair Chat*, 'the Great man of the Cats'. If both Gael and Norse equated cats with Picts, perhaps that is one reason for the animosity toward them, however deeply buried in folk memory.

This animosity took many forms, some of them particularly nasty. Well into the eighteenth century Highlanders attempted to gain powers by the ritual cat burning of Taighairm. In Skye this was known as 'giving the devil his supper' and the cat was roasted alive on a spit. The spectacle attracted other cats and if they suddenly became silent it was a sign that the Devil had arrived. He did not come as himself, but disguised as a cat, and if he could be knocked to the ground with a cross, or with the cross-hilt of a sword, he had to grant the cat roaster's wish.

A variation of this occurred in Glen Lyon, Perthshire as late as Halloween 1838, when a man disturbed a gathering of cats round the Clach Taghairm nan Chat, the Stone of the Devil Cat. On top of the stone sat a huge black cat and when the man appeared the black cat led an attack on him. Fighting furiously, the man reached the safety of a nearby house, but with a dead wildcat fastened to his back.

If cats escaped being roasted, they were still in danger, for they were once placed in the foundations of buildings in the belief that they kept away evil. The blood of a black cat could also he used as a hopeful cure for epilepsy, and if a cat ever became sick it was immediately taken outside and left alone. It was bad luck for a cat to die inside a house. Sometimes it was also bad luck to be a cat when moving house, for in Orkney it was believed that all the evil in the new house would enter the cat, killing it but leaving the people safe.

The native wildcats were, and are, formidable animals. Totally untameable unless caught newly born, they can stretch to over three feet in length and weigh 14 lbs. Their general fierceness earned it the nickname 'British tiger', but by the early decades of this century, the wildcat – *cat-findhaich* in Gaelic – seemed doomed to extinction. Treated more as vermin than game, keepers and sportsmen alike killed them as a matter of course and the few survivors huddled defiantly behind the barrier of Glen More.

The world wars, so destructive of other forms of life, saved them. Gamekeepers were valuable as fighting men, sportsmen were natural officer material and the wildcats gained the reprieve they needed.

Now they have spread, reclaiming the Highlands and striking south; sometime they might well be seen in the central belt, or among the hills and forests of Galloway.

One kind of cat which has also made the Highlands his own is the great Chattan Confederation of Badenoch. The Children of the Cat controlled Badenoch since the days of the Picts; perhaps they moved south from *Cataibh* when the Norse came; more likely they were always here. Their history is awesome both in depth and scope, with the *Toshach*, the original Headman, being *Gillechattan,* 'the cat-child', and their motto being 'touch not the cat but a glove' – in other words, don't meddle with Clan Chattan without adequate protection.

Good advice. Clan Chattan, comprising Mackintosh, Shaw, MacPherson, MacGillivray and Davidson, was quite capable of looking after itself. They fought the Norse in 1263, and Bannockburn, Harlaw and Culloden were among their battle honours. Twice there have been attempts to exterminate them: firstly by King James V, who commanded genocide against Clan Chattan with only the priests, women and children spared (they were to be exiled to Norway); and then by James Wolfe, who contemplated destroying all people bearing the name MacPherson.

Both attempts failed. The Mackintosh chief lives in Castle Moy in Badenoch and the people of Clan Chattan are widespread throughout the world. 'Touch not the cat but a glove.'

But it is as witches that cats are best known in Scottish folklore. In 1718 one William Montgomery spent many sleepless nights listening to the horde of cats which gathered at his door and spoke like humans. As the nights passed and the cats continued to cluster, Montgomery's patience broke and he rushed outside, flailing wildly with an axe. Two cats were killed, another injured, and next day Montgomery heard that two old women had been found dead and a third had a mysterious wound in her leg.

To us these myths of coincidence are a little absurd, a little amusing. To the people who had to live with those fears, these suspicions of every quiet moving feline, every bad tempered old woman, they were very real indeed. More importantly, the fear was real for Isobel Grierson of Prestonpans. She was burned at the stake on the Castlehill in Edinburgh in 1607 for, among other things, turning into a cat and creating havoc inside the house of Adam Clark.

Think of her, and the scores of others like her, who were killed for private superstition and public entertainment where today the pipes and drums march on the Castle esplanade – the poor unfortunates who were the living victims of irrational fear.

ELEVEN

THE DEVIL'S BREED

IF some birds were protected by their association with the Lord, many more were tainted by intimacy with the other side. Today most people listen quite happily to these birds, oblivious to the power of evil which flutters past with such seeming innocence.

Take the blackbird, whose sweet purity of song brings delight to the summer evening. Once this bird was an unsullied white, but winters were hard in the bad old days and it was caught in a storm. Rather than flee to the nearest tree, whose branches were swaying alarmingly in the blast, the whitebird flew into a solid looking chimney. It was warm there, and safe, until the bird learned that this was the devil's chimney. As the soot permeated his feathers, the whitebird knew that henceforth he would be known as the blackbird. Luckily, the quality of his song was not affected.

The wren is another perky little bird, jaunty with its upright tail and with a history as old as the Celts. Back in pre-Christian days, the Druids, white-robed Celtic priests of great learning and enigmatic power, used the wren in their divination. Apparently the Druids kept wrens as pets, which sits ill beside their game of hunt-the-wren in which a wren was pursued, caught and killed with branches of birch.

Because of its participation in druidic rites, the early Christians also hunted the inoffensive little wren and a Highland legend sprang up that it was a wren who told the Romans in which direction Christ had fled. (This was no doubt while Christ was perambulating around the Western Isles.)

The wren struck back with legends of its own. In Ayrshire and Galloway, killing a wren would cause cattle to produce blood instead of milk; and if a wren's nest was destroyed at the same time, the vandal would break a leg within a year. Another form of protection, or perhaps a carry-over from Druidical days, was the epithet the wren carried: Jenny Wren – 'Jenny' was another name for a witch.

Equally unpopular was the lapwing, known as a peewit or peezee, whose call of 'bewitched! bewitched!' unnerved the hearer. Everybody knew that this bird, with its undefinable colouring and mazy, irregular flight, held the departing soul of the dead. More practically, the peewit often alerted patrolling dragoons to the presence of hiding Covenanters – Presbyterians who refused to knuckle under and agree to the government of the day's insistence on Episcopalian worship. Instead they took to the hills of southern Scotland, worshipped in secret conventicles and defended themselves against all comers.

The Covenanters were ruthlessly persecuted, hunted, exiled, tortured and imprisoned by such people as Grierson of Lag, Lang Tam Dalyell and Bluidy Claver'se and they detested the peewit for its frequent circling of the hidden conventicles, places of worship, giving their enemies a clue as to their whereabouts. In the end, however, the Covenanters had their own triumph in the flame-scourged walls of Dunkeld, when a regiment of Cameronians, most devout of all Covenanters, defeated a rampant Episcopalian and Catholic army.

Less military than the peewit was the yellowhammer, known variously as the yorling, Scotch canary or yellow-yite. This bird haunts the hedgerows and its erratic flight and taunting whistle was blamed on the devil's blood which flowed through its veins. Because of this it was always tormented, its nests torn down and the fledglings killed. Yellowhammers were stoned in flight, their homes targeted for mere pastime and their song was supposed to be a devilish screech. Every May morning, the old proverb claimed, 'the yorling drinks a drop of the devil's blood'. (Incidentally, 1st May is the morning after Walpurgis night, Satan's birthday, but it is also Beltane, the old Celtic festival. How many of our superstitions reach back to the Celts?)

People claimed that the yorling's eggs were hatched by toads and some believed them the friend of the snake – itself a euphemism for the devil – or the Druids. The yorling carried food to the serpent and sometimes let the reptile eat its own young. As proof of this the yorling eggs have strange wavy lines on them, like snakes or the devil's writing.

Of course the yorling has the last word; listen to it as it flies tantalisingly close but always just out of reach. 'Whetil te! whetil te wheet!' the bird mocks – 'harry my nest and the de'il tak ye!'

Swifts and swallows are also birds of the devil. Swifts, referred to as 'souls of the damned', were sinful while human and have been damned to fly round the places they lived forever. Swallows are not quite the same. Their share of the devil's blood is carried under their tongue and only if they fall down a chimney in a shower of soot can they bring bad luck – a prophesy of death in some places. Homes without open fires seem to have built-in swallow insurance.

On the other hand, if a swallow builds its nest above a window it brings luck and prosperity to the house. To destroy the nest was to negate the luck and to risk a lot of evil within the year.

The wheatear is probably the most cursed of all the devil's brood. Like the yorling, its eggs are reputed to be hatched by toads and even to hear the short song brings bad luck, while to actually meet this quite attractive bird was certain death. Luckily they are not over common, thus saving a serious decline in Scotland's population.

In comparison it would be something of a relief to meet a curlew. Named a whaup in Scotland, this curve-billed bird lives in the moors and along the coast. Its eerie call brings a feeling of true loneliness to the fringes of the hill country and it has the courage, or instinct, to lure hunting foxes away from its nest. It is a beautiful bird to hear, but its name – whaup – had another meaning in Scotland. 'Whaup' was the name of a hook-nosed goblin which infested the gable end of houses; not a pleasant creature, but presumably only related to the curlew by the similarity of its nose.

Yet another bird with devil's blood under its tongue was the magpie. This bird has been cursed since the Ark when it was the same colour as the whitebird. While all the other birds followed Noah, the magpie remained outside to gibber and laugh at the flooding world. The magpie remained cantankerous at the Crucifixion when it refused to don full mourning plumage and was condemned to remain black and white until Doomsday.

Up in the north east knuckle of Buchan the magpie was the 'De'il's Bird', and if the reddest part of its tongue was cut and some human blood dropped in, it learned to speak. This might come in handy because many farmers used the magpie like a watchdog who gabbled at the approach of a stranger.

The magpie was unique in that different numbers seen meant different things. Various rhymes tell the story, but even the rhymes disagree. While one says:

Ane bodes grief, twa's a death,
Three's a wedding, four a birth.

Another will claim:

Ane's joy, twa's grief,
Three's a wedding, four a birth.

So it's best to pick the rhyme which suits the circumstance!

All Scotland seems to agree on this though: to invalidate the bad luck on seeing a magpie fly away from the sun, it was necessary to grab the first thing handy and throw it at the bird, saying 'bad luck to the bird that flies widdershins!'

However, that was unlikely to worry a bird cursed since the time of Christ.

TWELVE

AND A CUCKOO BROUGHT THE NEWS

MEN have always credited lesser animals with greater powers in forecasting both the weather and world events. Animals have been seen as messengers, oracles and luck-bringers, their behaviour watched, noted and divined. Conservation is lauded as a modern concept, yet the people of old Scotland held just about every creature in greater respect than we do now. Today the majority of people consider animals either as cute furry things or unique specimens to be protected simply because of their rarity. The people of old Scotland granted each form of creation more importance.

Take the eagle, most majestic of Scottish birds, denizen of the granite peaks and proud king of the clouds. Fine, but the folk who lived in the Shiant Islands, east of Lewis, knew all that and more. The Shiant are enchanted islands and it was believed that Adam and Eve had been changed into eagles and now lived on in the Highlands.

Given the great age of Adam and Eve it is not surprising that eagle feathers symbolised longevity, but that they also showed incorruptibility is interesting, remembering Eve's record with the forbidden fruit. Eagles' nests were protected by a curse, as whoever robbed them was condemned to a life without rest. Even so, many tried, for the rewards could be great.

Some nests held an eagle stone, a light brown aetite which was a powerful talisman against miscarriage and a general protection for pregnant women. It is easy to imagine a succession of worried young fathers-to-be scrambling down rock faces and up sheer cliffs to dare the anger of an eagle in an attempt to ease their wife's pregnancy. As it was Eve's misbehaviour which brought pain to childbirth, robbing her nest has its own irony.

There were other benefits from nest-robbing: if an eagle egg was shared between two people it was reckoned to protect against witchcraft, but that must be balanced against the bad luck occasioned by the robbery. And eagle's gall mixed with honey was supposed to cure bad eyesight, for those whose stomach was strong enough to cope!

In reality eagles are wary birds and easily frightened into deserting their eggs, which can then be stolen; while wrens often nest inside the eyrie of an eagle. So too do wildcats, but only after the eagle has left.

Eagles patrol large areas of sky in their quest for food, and they can lift fairly large creatures. Hares and fox cubs are favoured targets, or plover, ptarmigans, red deer calves and lambs. This made them enemies of man.

Like so many other creatures, they were

hunted by the Victorians whose sporting upper classes enjoyed nothing better than killing animals, counting the 'bag' and mounting the beast as a trophy of the hunt. In the island of Arran, the Duke of Hamilton ordered the annihilation of all eagles, and he was nearly successful. The golden eagle, the 'Great Beast' of the highlander, disappeared from the granite crags of Arran and the sole survivor was kept, chained in anguished slavery, for three decades. But now nature has triumphed, the eagle is back free on the soaring wind and funnelling on the updraught. Long may they stay.

In legend the eagle could also carry off children. There was a case in Unst, Shetland in 1790, when tiny Mary Anderson was left in the shelter of a bere or barley stook when her mother was in the house. An eagle saw the child, swooped and lifted her, shawl and all, into the air. Naturally there was consternation in Unst. William Anderson, the father, led a chase across the island, and when the eagle flew to nearby Fetlar he launched a boat and landed on the neighbouring island.

The Fetlar men were helpful, saying the bird was a white-tailed eagle and pointing out its nesting site on the high cliffs of Blue Banks. From the top of the cliff they could see nothing except a difficult overhang, but young Robert Nicholson from Southdale on Fetlar was lowered on the end of old ropes. To help him grip the rock, Robert's feet were painted with tar, and when he reached the eyrie Mary was still asleep with an eaglet on either side, their beaks entangled in her shawl. Robert freed her, brought her back to the top, and that was the end of that.

Or not quite. Many years later Robert was in Fetlar on an errand and he met Mary. As in all the best stories, they fell in love and got married. Their descendants still live on Shetland today.

Sometimes the eagle's burden was not so peaceful. There was the mysterious Ruaridh Troich, Rory the Dwarf, who was picked up from a point unknown while a baby and dropped at the equally obscure Dalnahaitnich. He became a feared archer who would have given Robin Hood a hard time, being able to fire one arrow into the air and split it clean through with a second. Given his turbulent start in life, it is amazing that Ruaridh did not become a full time eagle-hunter.

Another bird which mixed luck with message-carrying was the cuckoo, the gowk of Lowland Scotland. The cuckoo was not a popular bird, partly because of its habit of laying eggs in the nests of other birds, and partly because it was said to suck the eggs of smaller birds solely to beautify its own voice. Hunt the Gowk was the Scottish version of April Fool's Day, with a 'gowk' being another name for a fool. 'Ye daft gowk!' was a rebuke once frequently heard in many homes and schools.

Even so it is good luck to be outside when the first cuckoo of the year is heard and it is always a good idea to count the number of times the cuckoo calls. For every 'cuckoo!' heard, there is one year of life left for the listener. The cuckoos very presence announces the arrival of Spring, and once here the bird was believed to be a superb weather forecaster.

Again there are Scandinavian influences here: the cuckoo was known as the messenger of the god Thor, who brought thunder and storms. The cuckoo's song signified the coming of bad weather – known as a gowk-storm – or if it was heard during rain it meant that the weather would turn warm. Even so the Hebrideans deemed it unlucky to hear a cuckoo in the early morning and would expect a bad day in consequence.

On the Highland mainland the cuckoo was reputedly a friend of the fairy, spending Winter inside a *sithean*, a fairy dwelling.

St Kilda was for a long time the last outpost of Scotland, a misnamed scatter of islands cut off from Lewis by miles of rough Atlantic. The people here rarely saw a cuckoo and regarded it as a messenger bringing news of the death of their chief, MacLeod of Dunvegan. In February 1895 MacLeod did indeed die, but it was May before the factor sailed to St Kilda. He was surprised when the inhabitants knew of MacLeod's death, for there had been no communication with the islands in these pre-radio and telephone days. But birds could call, and a cuckoo had brought the news.

Animals also forecast the weather, and a quote from *Poor Robin's Almanack* of 1733 is worth repeating. Robin claimed to be a knight from Burntisland in Fife.

> *Observe which way the hedgehog builds her nest,*
> *To front the north or south, or east or west;*
> *For if 'tis true that common people say,*
> *The wind will blow the quite contrary way.*

Poor wee hedgehog: this skill is nearly forgotten today and these tiny animals are more often seen scurrying for cover from the racing wheels of a high powered motor car. Perhaps if we granted the hedgehog a little more respect, we might save some vulnerable animal lives.

THIRTEEN

A SOO'S TAIL TO YE!

THERE would be drovers in their heavy homespun, with the tarnished silver belt buckle which ensured they would never lie in a pauper's grave. There would be tinkers plying their trade, hammers beating rhythmically on metal utensils, and muggers selling their wares. There would be cottagers with their wives, and hinds with their bondagers. There would be millers, prosperous and unpopular, a recruiting sergeant in red coat and black boots, ready to slip the King's shilling into the glass-bottomed tankard of an unwary youth. There would be servants and serving wenches, herds and proud gentlemen, horses and cattle and sheep. Most of all there would be sheep, for this was the Linton Market, the largest sheep market in Scotland.

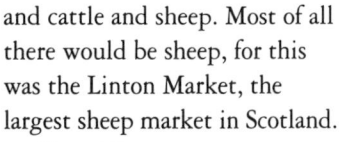

For well over a century Linton Roderick, now known less poetically as West Linton, was the focal point for the sheepmen of southern Scotland, so much so that the sheep sold here came to be known as Linton

Sheep. The breed still exists – only the name has changed – and black-faced sheep can be seen nearly everywhere in the country.

There are a couple of theories concerning the origin of the Scottish black-faces. King James IV was given the credit for bringing a flock to the Ettrick Forest in the borders back in 1503, and if it was not him, why not blame the ships of the 1588 Spanish Armada? However, it is unlikely that either theory is correct.

According to Michael Robson of Newcastleton in Liddesdale, who is an authority on the subject, the black-faced sheep probably evolved over centuries of breeding from many local varieties. Furthermore, Mr Robson argues that nearly every area of Scotland would once have had its own breed, which is a theory strengthened by looking at the island sheep.

The Orkney strain are based mainly on North Ronaldsay in the north east of the island group and seem to thrive in the exposed conditions. Because of their diet of seaweed, they are frequently referred to as the 'seaweed eating sheep'. Only the ewes and lambs feed on grass, and then for a short three months in the year. They are attractive sheep, with every colour of fleece from black to brown, fawn and white.

St Kilda is often thought of as a romantic place, perhaps mainly by people who have never considered a North Atlantic winter with its long dark nights, short dark days and nearly unremitting foul weather. Yet in a way there is romance in this outpost of Scotland with its unique fauna and incredible cliffs. It was here that the Soay sheep survived, and from here they spread. Soay is a tiny island in the group and the Soay sheep are not large but are very hardy and moult away their hard wool in summer. Agile and ancient, they have endured since Neolithic times and hopefully will continue to do so.

The St Kilda sheep does not only come from St Kilda, but from anywhere in the Hebrides, hence their old – and more accurate – name of Hebridean sheep. No doubt they had other names before that, when they were introduced by the Norse. As a rare breed they are not so rare today, but are still interesting with long soft hair, dark faces, wicked eyes and spectacularly curved horns.

Although fascinating to look at, these ancient breeds are virtually useless as a commercial proposition, except to attract visitors. The black-faced sheep rules the Scottish hills, thriving on the bleak hill land of Scotland from Cheviot to Harris – and still, after so long, not always accepted. To John Muir, the Dunbar-born conservationist who invented the concept of National Parks, sheep were 'hoofed locusts'.

Sheep do graze away much of the variety from the hillsides. They can overgraze, they do have a tendency to create a mono-culture of treeless grass – but they also enable people to live in the upland areas. In other words, without sheep you have a mono-culture of grassless trees, and peopleless hills.

Or, would there be a return to the old days? Before sheep, the valleys and particularly the Highland glens were home to entire communities – mixed communal farming with crops and cattle and traditions which reached into the far past. Defeat of the Jacobites in 1746 led to the loss of the chief's power and consequent loss of the chief's need of his clan. Bankruptcy and the subsequent 'Clearances' followed to make the glens more profitable. Out went the people, in came the sheep.

This is a very simplified history. Harking back to the good old days is profitless, for were they so good? Could we ever have retained the people in the glens? And, more importantly, would people want to return to subsistence agriculture with its associated hardships and uncertainties? Unlikely – yet there is fertile ground, and land which could be made fertile, and populated, in the empty glens – glens which were 'cleared' for sheep and are now used for deer-stalking. Ireland has a populated countryside; why not Scotland?

Although sheep have long been part of the Scottish scene, they do not have the same attraction for superstition as cattle. If, for example, a flock was milling around, or bleating for no obvious reason, it was a sign of approaching bad weather. There is also a connection with the old religion, for if a sheep miscarried, the dead lamb was put on a rowan tree – a sacred tree – to prevent miscarriage in the remainder of the flock. More conventionally, it is bad luck to drive or walk through a flock on the road – remembering the nervous nature of sheep, this is just common sense, and anyway the shepherd might object.

The shepherd might also have objected to the old seers, who scraped the flesh from the shoulder blade of a black sheep, threw it in the fire and told the future by the resulting cracks. But Highland shepherds also had their superstitions: lambs were always marked on St Columba's day, a Thursday, and the piece cut from their ear was buried where it could not be dug up by an animal. The plant which grew above the cut piece was hung above the lamb to protect it through life.

There were other methods of protecting sheep. Using an ash wood crook helped, for it was believed that animals could not be injured by ash. Shepherds also burned away the hair round the base of a lamb's neck to prevent death by pine marten. This engaging but quite rapacious animal is related to the weasel and lives on anything from berries to hares, although it is said to enjoy raspberry jam. Unfortunately the pine marten also hunts game birds and was suspected of killing lambs by jumping up, lodging its claws in the lamb's fleece and biting its throat. Hence the actions of Highland shepherds.

Pine martens themselves have been in danger, but again the chief predator has been man. Professional hunters attempted their extermination, forests were cut or burned down and its fur was valued for export.

However, the marten survived and this century it began to expand its territory, recrossing the Great Glen on its southward march. Someday it might be numerous enough for shepherds again to shave the neck fleece of their lambs.

Another unpopular animal in the Highlands was the pig, possible because it was once sacred. The early Christian missionaries could have been responsible for this change of heart, as the pig became an unlucky animal, tainted with the devil's mark on his fore trotters. Pigs had weather associations, mainly bad: a pig with a straw in his mouth meant foul weather and they could scent a coming gale. They were also connected with thunder and lightning and so were unpleasant to have around.

In pre-Christian days, pork was meat for warriors, with the greatest hero choosing the prime piece, and alcoholic drink consumed in great quantity. This combination could lead to violence, if there was a pretender to the hero's crown and the ale was plentiful. In later days there was a revulsion against pork and it was never to be served at a wedding.

Fishermen throughout Scotland did not like pigs. There were no half measures; among other things pigs were known as 'grunters', and if they were referred to by name while at sea it brought bad luck. Calling 'soo's tail to ye!' to a Fife fisherman was a terrible insult ('soo' is a sow). Once at Buckhaven a mischievous boy threw a pig's tail onto a fishing boat as it left the harbour. The boat returned to her berth, remaining there all day. No doubt the boy was summarily dealt with.

But pigs had one good quality: bathing in their blood was supposed to cure warts.

FOURTEEN

FABULOUS BEASTS

THERE are various types of kelpie, water horses, seacattle and water bulls; there are mermaids and fairy dogs and other unspecified monsters. Scottish folklore is saturated with them. Best known of all is the Loch Ness Monster, familiarly known as 'Nessie', which has existed from at least the time of St Columba to the present day. Columba had sent one of his monks, Lugne Mocomin, to swim the Ness and fetch a boat. Then Nessie appeared. That was no problem for Columba, who sent the beast back and made the sign of the cross to ensure it kept its distance in future.

Another story puts things in a different light. Rather than attacking the missionaries, the monster ferried them to the Pictish capital near Inverness. In return Columba granted Nessie a soul and the freedom of the loch. Obviously Nessie appreciated the gift for she still swims around, surfacing only to wave to sundry camera-less passers-by. Interestingly, the name 'Ness' means 'Roaring One', so perhaps the monster was known even before the sixth century.

The locals knew of its presence last century, long before the present sixty year old spate of monster sightings. At that time it was referred to as the 'Loch Ness Shark'.

Probably the next best known 'thing' is the Grey Man of Ben MacDhui in the Cairngorms. This is a ten foot tall, man-shaped creature which has been felt following hillwalkers the eleven miles to Braemar. Some accounts are ludicrous, saying that the Grey Man wore a top hat; others have put a more sinister interpretation on the beastie, with psychic reactions and the sound of heavy footsteps. In *Fear Liath Mor*, the big Grey Man, do we perhaps have a relative of Bigfoot? Or some other ancient spectre of the hills?

If it seems unlikely that any large mammal could remain undiscovered and relatively unseen in such a small country as Scotland, remember that the Cairngorms can be a strange and lonely place. Rather than criticise from an armchair, better to try a solo walk up Ben MacDhui, listen awhile … and wonder.

Water horses and water bulls have similar traits – both appear like an animal but are larger; both are often black or dark green; and both capture stray people and haul them into whichever loch or river they inhabit. This is by day. By night the water bull, and particularly the water horse, transforms into a sleek and handsome young man who is very attractive to young women. The rest of the story is obvious: the courtship, the walk by the loch, the change into a horse or bull – and the drowning and eating. One way of checking to see if a horse is one of these so-called kelpies is to scratch its head – which they enjoy, by the way. If there is sand or seaweed there, run!

Once there was a Badenoch youth who met a beautiful and extremely friendly young woman. Too friendly perhaps and the couple became a topic of local gossip. One night they went for their habitual walk, laughing and joking together, when the girl threw back her head and laughed. For an instant the youth listened, then he realised that the laugh had changed into a loud neigh. Reaching inside his plaid, he drew out his dirk and stabbed her to death. She collapsed at his feet, a dark green water horse with the seaweed tangled round her head.

Sometimes a pretty maiden could charm a water horse – *an each uisge* in Gaelic – into wearing a bridle with a cross shape cut into the cheek. This enslaved the kelpie so he had to work for the maiden. The Pondage Kelpie was captured this way and made to build Morphie Castle. On release he cursed the castle:

> *Sair's my back and sair's my banes*
> *Cairtin' the Laird o' Morphy's stanes*
> *So long as the Pondage Kelpie's alive*
> *The Keep o' Morphy'll never thrive.*

It didn't. There is nothing left of the castle.

Kelpies, particularly in the eastern Lowlands north of Dundee – the old heartland of the Picts – seem to have been prone to capture, and many bridges, mills and even some churches are attributed in part to them.

So Kelpies, in some form, were a pan-Celtic beast and were not confined solely to the Gaelic areas of Scotland.

Perhaps there is some relation between the kelpie and the old river spirits which claim a certain number of victims annually. The best known example is in the rhyming exchange between the Tweed and the Northumbrian Till:

> *Tweed said to Till:*
> *'What gars ye rin sae still?'*
> *Till said to Tweed:*
> *'Though ye rin wi' speed,*
> *An' I rin slaw,*
> *For ilka man ye droon,*
> *I droon twa.'*

An old Mingulay farmer faced a more solid entity when he found a strange cow in with his herd. He was an honest man, so he searched for her owner, but without success. Finally he kept the cow, which was both a prolific milker and a bearer of excellent calves. As the years passed the farmer's entire herd was bred from the one cow, but she was ageing and he told his wife that she was due to be slaughtered.

At dawn the next day the cow walked to the shore, followed by all her offspring. Instead of stopping at the water's edge they walked straight in and disappeared.

They were sea cattle, but there were also fairy cattle, *crodh sith*, who were normally dun-coloured and hornless, except on Skye where they were red or speckled. Whatever colour though, they all ate seaweed. Tales of these creatures were most prevalent in Skye, Harris and Tiree.

Much more romantic than kelpies or cattle are the mermaids, the *maighdean chuain* who haunted our shores. In popular imagination the mermaid is usually seen just offshore, combing her long hair while sitting on a rock, which is exactly what William Munro, schoolmaster at Reay, saw at the back end of the eighteenth century.

In his own words:

> ... *my attention was arrested by the appearance of a figure, resembling an unclothed female, sitting upon a rock extending into the sea, and apparently in the action of combing its hair, which flowed around its shoulders, and of a light brown colour.*

He watched this figure for only a few minutes, as it soon returned to the sea.

Mr Munro wrote twelve years after the event to support another sighting in Caithness, when a human-like creature was seen floating face up in the waves. No tail was observed, but witnesses, including the daughter of a minister, had no need to fabricate the story. Nor had John McIsaac of Kintyre who told a hearing that on the 18th October 1811 he saw something on a rock, the top half of which was white and human shaped, the lower half 'of a brindled or reddish grey colour, apparently covered with scales, but the extremity of the tail itself was of a greenish red shining colour'. Again the creature had long, light brown hair, but this time it remained on the rock for about two hours.

Mermaids have also been seen in this century: Sandy Gunn of Sutherland found one in Sandwood Bay in 1900, another was seen near Muck in the mid 1940s. The years are interesting – 1790s, 1811, 1900, 1940s – all these sightings were during times of political unrest. French wars, Boer War, World War. Does man's emotional upheaval call up some supernatural creature, a spectator from a watery ethereal plane? Or is it just coincidence?

What cannot be coincidence are the mysterious cat-like creatures which are continually seen throughout Scotland, at the same time as sheep are killed. In the 1970s and early 1980s an unknown beast stalked the far north, from Bonar Bridge to Strathy but notably around Bettyhill. This became known as the Skerray Beast. Various people saw – something – in the lonely hill country, and there were many theories: was it a puma, a hyena or a lynx? An escaped zoo animal, an escaped pet, a native Scottish lynx? Or something else?

The lynx was once common to Scotland and remains have been found in Sutherland. More recently, and more disturbingly, in 1975 a lynx was caught in a fox snare in Moray, a thousand years and more after the lynx supposedly became extinct in Scotland.

And then, in the summer of 1994, a pair of large golden brown animals with black plumes on their ears were seen south of Hawick. This was no sighting by casual tourists fresh from the city, but by experienced forestry workers. So it was not a fox or large dog but something else. A lynx? Or are there still kelpies out there in the Scottish countryside … ?

FIFTEEN

HORNY GOLOCHS AND TODDLER TYKES

IT is a well known story, how Robert The Bruce was sheltering in his cave when he saw the wyver. He was in Arran, or possibly Carrick or even Rathlin – the location does not matter – and the English were searching for him. His enemies were in the ascendancy, his forces had been shattered and his hope was nearly gone; and then he saw the wyver.

It was just a normal wee wyver, nothing fancy – eight-legged, wriggly, crawling up the rocky wall. Suddenly it fell. So it tried to swing to a ledge on the opposite corner to put up a strand of its web, and it fell again. So it tried again, and fell again. By now Robert The Bruce was interested in the trials of this persistent wyver, and he watched as it kept trying, again and again. At last it succeeded, and Bruce was pleased. So pleased that he grasped his sword, strode out and won Scotland's crown for himself.

Generations of children must have heard that story, except that the wyver was Anglicised to a spider. Same beastie, same result, different name. But that is typical of Scotland: most of our insect names have been forgotten, even though they are every bit as correct and frequently more descriptive than the English alternatives.

Wyvers, or spiders, have always been well regarded in Scotland, perhaps because they slaughter midges, or maybe because of that early encounter with royalty, and to find one in the house is regarded as good luck.

Even better luck is to have a money spider running across a coat or shirt while it was being worn, for that meant new clothes were on their way. If put in a wallet, the money spider brought wealth. Naturally, people seldom killed a spider: 'If ye wish to live lang and thrive, Let a spider run alive,' said the old rhyme. However, that was surely contradicted by the old fever cure, which consisted of placing a live spider in a nutshell and hanging the shell around the sufferer's neck. Yet again, if a spider was killed deliberately, the killer made a point of breaking some crockery or glassware that same day.

Spiders' webs came in handy too, as an antiseptic bandage which was placed on a cut. Perhaps there was a holy quality about the web, for when Baby Christ was hidden from the Romans, a spider spun its web round Him so He could not be seen.

Spiders could also cure thrush, this time by being enclosed in a goose quill – no wonder they try to scurry away whenever a human being appears on the scene.

That other popular creature, the snail, also produced an effective medicine. Snail slime was a panacea which not only cured tuberculosis, but also whooping cough and gout.

Added to that, it could be used to determine a future spouse. Just place a snail in a bowl on Halloween and next morning it will have written the initials of the wife- or husband-to-be. Remember to place the bowl upside down though, or the snail will escape.

If a spider was known as a 'wyver', and a 'goloch' was the genetic term for any insect, then a 'horny goloch' had to be an earwig (although it was also known as a 'clipshear', or a 'clippie', or even a 'clippie forkie' which is really a good name for the disgusting little brutes). Another descriptive name was the 'De'il's darning needle' for a dragonfly, although again in some areas this could be the 'Lord's darning needle'. And a 'slater' is definitely a nice flat-sounding name for that prehistoric survivor – the woodlouse.

But don't forget the 'bumclock'. What an elegant name for a beetle, even if legend did say they could create a fit in highly strung women. Beetles were well protected, for if one was killed it brought either rain or the whole gamut of storms, thunder and lightning. And if by any chance a beetle was found lying on its back, it was good luck to replace it on its feet.

On the opposite end of the popularity scale, the butterfly was seen as a symbol of the soul and if one was met flying at night it was a warning of coming death. The Gaels believed that a butterfly above a corpse was the soul hovering, and if the butterfly was gold, it pointed to a happy life in the hereafter.

And then there was the ladybird, the red and black polka-dotted beetle which even adults like to see. It was unlucky to kill these little insects and instead girls held them between cupped hands, said: 'Fly away east or fly away west, And show me where lives the one I like best' – before releasing it. The ladybird would obey, flying in the direction the girl, perhaps inadvertently, had pointed her hands towards.

Bees too could fly in a straight line, and if they chose to come directly toward someone's face, that meant good news was on the way. Away out west on Uist the first bumble bee of spring always brought good luck and could be treated in various ways: for heavy fleece on the sheep the bee should be placed in the wool bag; to ensure prosperity the bee should be placed in a purse; and for a contented life the bee should be left in the house.

However, bees don't always bring good luck. If an unclaimed swarm set up home on someone's property it was considered bad luck; and while other animals kneel or call at midnight on Christmas Eve, the bee has to rise at three on Christmas morning, only to leave the hive and return immediately. Not much luck for them in that, is there?

It was a Fife man, John Gedde from Falkland, who invented the modern concept of a beehive, back in 1668. His idea was to have an octagonal wooden box with carrying handles and an internal fixed framework for honeycombs. With a second, similar, box added, the majority of bees clustered round the queen in one box, leaving the second relatively free, which facilitated the removal of the honeycomb. Prior to this, beekeepers picked the hive, straw skeps only, which had the highest yield and killed the bees to take the honey. This was a system which was both cruel and wasteful as the best bees were exterminated. Gedde was granted a royal patent for his invention, and he also wrote the first Scottish beekeeping manual in 1675. The world began to take note of Scottish beekeeping.

And, naturally, the Scots had their own name for bees, which were regarded as the tiny winged servants of God. What was known south of Cheviot as the 'bumble bee' was known here as the 'bumbee', 'donner bee' or the evocative 'toddler tyke'. Then there was the 'fuggie-toddler', the small, yellowy orange bee, and the 'rid-beltie' which is obviously the bee with a red stripe. The 'rid-doup' is equally clear, a bee with a red dowp, or bottom, and the 'garrie bee' has black and yellow stripes. Quite a collection for a humble bee, and no doubt there were plenty more.

In legend the bee was not always so colourful. In the beginning they were white, but when Eve munched on her piece of fruit the bee turned brown. They are a Christian creature, in spite of having to rise at three in the morning, and worship with their buzz, only humming Psalm 100 on Christmas Eve. Perhaps because of this bees are renowned for their wisdom and will sting anyone they consider blasphemous. They will also flee the hive if they suspect anger or hatred, stopping on the way to severely sting an adulterer. However, they will leave a maiden unharmed, even if she walks right through a swarm.

Obviously every wife and mother of daughters hoped for a beehive for her birthday.

A lone bee entering a house should always be allowed to leave unmolested, and if it lands on somebody's head, money is coming. Even a bee sting is no bad thing, for it is meant to cure rheumatism, and bees should never be kept in ignorance. If there is anything in the offing – a birthday, marriage, even a minor dispute – the bees in the local hive should be informed, for they are part of the family and should be treated as such.

One man who knew this was John Moir, whose vast collection of beekeeping books has been retained in the George IV Bridge library in Edinburgh. They include the manual by John Gedde and the 1747 book of Robert Maxwell, *The Practical Bee Master*. For those interested in bees, it is worth a visit.

SIXTEEN

BEARS IN THE BADGER'S FORD

IN our present age where reliance on technology is overwhelming, it is sometimes difficult to realise how important animals once were in everyday life. Yet there is evidence of this all around us in the names of features and places which are passed, visited, walked over and occasionally worshipped and reviled.

These names invade modern life and are used without thought in everyday speech – examples of our inescapable association with the past. Edinburgh is blessed with such reminders, particularly the older parts of the city. Take the Cowgate, which runs parallel to the High Street in the heart of the Old Town. Although under some development today this is still a rather sad street lined with grimy houses, 1960s University buildings and a church – but once it was a busy thoroughfare for cattle.

The Cowgate runs from Holyrood to the Grassmarket – both have animal associations. The Grassmarket was where Lothian farmers brought their hay and corn to sell to the merchants in the city. In Holyrood Park there is a

Hunters Bog, a natural trap in the days when Scottish kings chased the deer.

Still in Edinburgh, 'The Sheep's Head' – locally pronounced 'Heid' – is an ancient inn at Duddingston which for centuries specialised in serving a boiled sheep's head to hungry diners. Perhaps not such a popular dish today, a sheep's head was once fairly common on the table. Indeed James VI bestowed a ram's head, suitably decorated, to the inn back in 1580.

Such an item is not part of the current menu, but fashions can change and perhaps it will be reinstated in the future.

Sometimes places have essentially kept the same names, but the passage of years has eroded the meaning. Roxburgh is a prime example of this. There are three places of this name: Roxburgh the county, Roxburgh the village and Roxburgh the capital of Scotland. The county has vanished, to be replaced by a district of the same name; the village, which probably predates the county, has survived; and the capital is virtually forgotten.

A few walls remain, overgrown, crumbling, but even these formed part of the once royal castle. Churches, markets, workshops and houses, all have vanished yet the name remains – Roxburgh. Once it was Rokesburgh; and before that, Rooksburgh. Here the kings of Scots held court, here the royal mint produced money for the realm, here were markets and priests, streets and families, and here a king died when his own cannon exploded. All where the rooks once were and are again on a summer evening. Royal Roxburgh has now been returned to the rooks from whom it gained its name.

Sometimes the names have a poetry which disguises the brutality of history. Caerlaverock is a name whose syllables can be rolled round the mouth and savoured, yet one which would be spat out as a curse 1400 years back. Caerlaverock was the 'fort of the laverock' or lark. Once, when the old forces of paganism were rallied to face the march of the Lord, this place near the Solway Firth, then known as the Sea of Rheged, provided the excuse for a battle.

Or so the legends say: 'For a lark's nest' the battle of Arthuret was fought, when the Celtic armies clashed in AD 573 and Rhydderich Hen emerged as the victor. It was a fratricidal war, Briton against Briton. Afterwards Myrddyn, possibly the original of the Arthurian Merlin, ran to the forest of Caledon to live in the wilds until his legendary death at Drumelzier. Rhydderich, the King of Strathclyde, was guided by St Kentigern, who founded Glasgow Cathedral and brought a robin back to life. This all but forgotten battle pushed the borders of Christianity southward, toward the advancing pagan Angles.

There is a castle today at Caerlaverock, but it is mediaeval, highly photogenic and has nothing whatsoever to do with the 'lark's nest' of Myrddyn. But here too there was a battle, when Edward I of England led his armies north to squash the Scots. Caerlaverock fell, after a siege which was remembered in verse, but the Scots refused to lie down and instead of victory Edward's invasion caused the rise of Robert The Bruce.

Some names are different but have the same meaning. Penicuik is a major town in Midlothian, sprawling along the flat lands beside the Pentland Hills; while Gowkshill is a tiny community of three streets and one shop, also in Midlothian but about six miles to the north east. Both names mean the same thing; *Pen -y -cuik* is from the Celtic 'hill of the cuckoos', while *gowk* is Scots for a cuckoo.

And so we have two Cuckoo hills only a few miles apart, but once divided by language and culture. If nothing else, this shows how little these things – race, culture, language – really matter. All merge in time, and with the Pentland Hills meaning the 'hills of the Picts', nearby Newtongrange having Saxon roots, and Gorebridge coming from the Gaelic *gabhar*, a goat, 'bridge of goats' – the area is a cultural hodge-podge.

Other places are easily misconstrued: take the Brig o' Turc in the Trossachs. The initial image is of an inhabitant of Turkey crossing the bridge; but *turc* is Gaelic for a boar, as in *Carn an Torc*, 'hill of the boar' in Deeside. At one time boars were widespread throughout Scotland and no doubt these names date back for centuries.

This also holds true for Baudy Meg which is a hill in Deeside. Who was Meg? And why and how was she bawdy? Unfortunately there never was such a person; Baudy Meg is a corruption of the Gaelic *Badan Magh*, 'hill of hares', which is not nearly such an interesting name, even if it is more accurate.

Hare hills are quite common in South Scotland: the Pentland Hills have one, as well as a Bawdy Moss; there is a Hareburn and a Harehope in Tweeddale; a Hareshaw in the Cheviots and another near Kilmarnock. But a wee word of caution here: with hares so often being mistaken for witches, these hare connections might just have a double meaning. And given the lewd behaviour of witches, there might have been a Bawdy Meg after all!

There could also be some ambiguity about Glen and Loch Iorsa in Arran. The name seems straightforward enough – 'loch of the snake' or 'adder' – but it is a damp, dark, boggy place and adders like a nice sunny rock to curl up on. However, Glen Iorsa is also very atmospheric; there is a stillness here, a sense of menace, and the surface of the loch is dark, mysterious. Could it be that the snakes were in fact Druids? Arran certainly has an excess of ancient religious sites, some very close by. It is not a possibility to dismiss lightly.

Creag nan Fitheach is in Colonsay, *Beinn na Fithlach* on Islay – and both refer to ravens. Ravens, the sign of the Norse and these features, rock and hill, are more likely to refer to the Vikings than to the birds. They are a stark reminder of the long occupation of much of Scotland by the Scandanavians. For 400 years the high-prowed ships prowled the Scottish seas and the sign of the raven brought fear, slavery and death. Somerled wrenched open the iron jaws of the dragon in two sea fights off Islay and the raven limped, broken winged, to tend its wounds.

There is one animal based place name which is used daily by thousands of people and it is doubtful if even one per cent are aware of its meaning. Ibrox Park, home of Rangers Football Club, is one of the most famous football grounds in Europe. Rangers have maintained a consistently high success rate since their foundation, winning both domestic and European honours. In Scotland they are known as the 'Bears', but the name is a misnomer – for Ibrox means 'ford of the badgers'.

Perhaps Rangers should change their famous blue strip for one of black and white and alter their name to the 'Badgers'.

Perhaps not! The 'Glasgow Badgers' – somehow it doesn't have quite the same ring.

SEVENTEEN

HERALDIC ANIMALS

POCKETS of mist checkered the countryside of Northern England as the army plodded on. There was banter in the air, the Norman French of the iron knights as cheerful as the Gaelic and Scots of their rough clad footmen. Banners hung limp so their bold, still crude, symbols were only partly visible. Heraldry in all its forms, with its rigid structure and formal French language, was still evolving from its birthplace in Outremer, the Holy Land, but animals had been used on banners for centuries, perhaps millennia.

There had been the eagle of Rome, which had spread its wings as the city spread her conquests, and the talons had gripped fast and held wherever the wing shadows fell. Except Scotland. North of the wall of Hadrian, and especially beyond the turf rampart of Antonine, the eagle banners were obscured in the mists, tattered by the forests and nibbled by the terrible midges of Caledonia.

After the eagle came the dragon, coiling above the marching lines of Angle and Saxon as they advanced paganism and the Germanic cultures against Caledonia, or Alba. With the same result: the dragon banner meant no quarter would be given, and in a series of thrusts which began at the time of King Arthur, the frontier was fluid and bloody.

Some of these encounters have been remembered – Dagestan when Aidan of Dalriada led his Scots to halt the Anglian advance; Cattraeth when a raiding party of Celts from Lothian was slaughtered to the last man; Nechtansmere where the Picts threw back the Anglians and the border recoiled to the line of Forth and Clyde, to be further shoved southward by the battle of Carham on the Tweed.

These same Picts are one of the enigmatic races of history. At one time they probably held all Scotland north of, and including, the central belt, but they were concentrated in the fertile crescent which curved from Fife to Caithness. Not much is known about the Picts, but they showed superb skill in stone carving, endured as a race for centuries and possibly fought under the banner of a boar.

It is likely that they eventually amalgamated with the Scots rather than surrendered to them, but there were still periods of intense warfare. In one of these the Picts captured DunAdd. This Argyll hill-fort was the capital of Scottish Dalriada and on the solid weathered rock there is a carving of a boar. Was this a taunting celebration of victory? Or a mason's casual whim, much like the 'Kilroy was here' or spray-painted walls of modern gang warfare. Which brings us to the question: were these Dark Age heroes so heroic, or has history transformed local gangsters into something grander, glossed over by time and distance?

Somewhere among this mayhem came the most famous gangsters of all, the Vikings. Ravens replaced dragon and eagle and boar, and the sea was a highway of horror. Romans, Saxon, Norse, the legions of terror broke in successive waves against the rocks of Alba. Broke and dissipated, merged and fought, amalgamated and loved and sang and settled until Pict and Scot became one with Angle and Briton and Norseman, until the nation of Scotland was forged. The race was proud but strangely gentle, imbued with the mysticism of sea and hill and the hard-headed love of the soil, a people whose myriad banners had met in conflict and who now recognised just one symbol above them all.

Only one beast was powerful enough to control this quarrelsome breed, and the Scots chose the king of beasts to roar them on. The lion. The Rampant Lion of Royal Scotland.

But was this a Norman-French introduction to Scotland? Or was it so much older than that, belonging on this soil as a banner certainly, if never as a beast? Away back before the Normans, before even the Vikings, legend tells of a Scottish force serving with the great Emperor Charlemagne. Acting as bodyguard to the Emperor, this force could have been the precursor of the Auld Alliance with France, or merely a foretaste of the Scottish mercenary tradition, but they fought under the lion banner. It is said that Charlemagne (771-814) allowed a Scottish king to use French lilies as 'a defence to the lion of Scotland' as the Scots soldiers defended him.

Then there was the Lion of Galloway. A strange province, Galloway was named after the *Gallgael*, the foreign Gaels. A hybrid race of Norse and Gael and no doubt Britons, they were once wholly independent. There were clans here, a host of fighting men who raised armies and launched fleets. One of their Lords was Alan, and he flew a Lion flag. The Lion of Galloway was a mean cat to cross.

Later came William the Lion, King of Scots. Although with more Gaelic blood than Norman, William aped the manners of Normandy. The iron knights were rulers of Europe, the Church of Rome was dominant and the lords and kings of Christendom fell in obedient line. From her lowland heartland, Norman Scotland expanded, annexing Galloway, subduing Moray and taming Ross. William was instrumental in the latter and his methods were crudely Norman and won the respect of his peers. 'Friend of God' they termed him, and 'the Lion of Justice'.

And so it was William's army which found itself lost in the Northumbrian mist that fateful day, marching southwards. Warfare then was brutal but was a way of life to these knights. They enjoyed the sport of slaughter and their ballads rang with the pleasure of butchery. William saw what he thought was a party of his own men coming through a rent in the mist and he advanced toward them. Too late he realised they were English, the enemy, but instead of withdrawing, a sensible response, he couched lance and charged.

For a knight errant it would have been rash but praiseworthy, but for a king it was crass stupidity and very costly. William was unhorsed, captured and forced to ransom Scotland to pay for his freedom. A lion of justice he might have been, but in battle William displayed the characteristics of a lemming rushing to pointless destruction.

But Scotland survived, just, and so did the lion. Alexander the Second, son of William, rode under a lion rampant – a lion standing upright on its hind legs – when he retook Argyll from Norway; and his son, Alexander III, developed the lion rampant theme further until it became more recognisable to the one we know today – the Royal Red Lion. And the lion flicked his mighty paw and called up a storm which lost the Vikings the battle of Largs in 1263.

It was of this banner that William Dunbar, the sixteenth century poet, wrote:

This awful beast was terrible of cheir,
Piercing of look and stout of countenance,
Right strang of corps in fashion fair but fier,
Lusty of shape, light of deliverance;
Red of his colour as the ruby glance.
On field of gold he stood full mightily
With fleur de lis circled pleasantly.

It was sometimes the continuation of the nation herself. During the long Wars of Independence, Stirling Castle was the key to Scotland, the keep at the crossroads between South and North, Lowlands and Highlands, Forth and Clyde. William Wallace defeated

Hugh de Cressingham at Stirling Brig and lost Falkirk a few miles to the east and it was for Stirling that Bruce fought Bannockburn.

In 1304 the castle was under English siege. A small band of patriots defended the walls, throwing back attack after attack, enduring the pinching agony of famine, the thump and thunder of the great war engines. Throughout that grim period a single standard fluttered above the noise and stench and dust – the Lion Rampant.

There was no king, for John Balliol had abdicated and Bruce had yet to declare himself; Wallace was a hunted fugitive and there seemed no hope, no point in continuing.

So then came the question to the gallant defenders: 'For whom do you fight? Of whom do you hold the castle?'

And Sir William Oliphant, the Perthshire knight, pointed to the red roaring lion.

'Of the Lion!' he replied.

EIGHTEEN

TRAVELLERS AND FLYING MONKS

THE Celts were always a wandering people and there were always wandering people among the Celts. From the plains of eastern Europe, through Bavaria to Iberia and Ireland, the Celtic people moved, the wagons lifting the dust of travel and their passage marked by artefacts, bloodlines and story.

As they stabilised with the general coalescence of Europe, some merged with different races to form countries; but others remained on the road, perennial nomads and itinerant journeymen. These became the travelling people, the 'gaun-about-folk' to the Scottish Lowlanders, who formed clans like the tinker MacPhees and tinker Stewarts. And in time they were joined by Romanies from Asia.

While they travelled they evolved a culture of their own, associated with but separate from the settled communities through which they passed. They also amassed a fund of lore.

At midnight on Christmas Eve every donkey in the world knelt down in honour of the birth of Christ. This fact can be ascertained by examination of the donkey's knees: the black patches arrived when the first donkey knelt down to Jesus.

One dark December night, when the stars were hidden by cloud and the ground was wet with rain, an old tramp was searching for shelter. He followed a drystane dyke, nearly bumped his head on a notice board and walked into a byre which had been left open. It was warmer inside and the tramp sighed gratefully, burrowing into a pile of straw and trying to sleep.

There were sounds outside, the tramping of hooves and a low snort, and the tramp looked up to see something bulky blocking the barn entrance. Again that snort, a deafening bellow and the tramp felt a quiver of fear – it was a bull! There was nowhere to hide, nowhere to run and the bull was just inside the entrance, pawing the ground, with its head lowered. It was silhouetted thus against the sky just as a star appeared through a rent in the clouds; a bright star which seemed to move, opening up the whole of heaven.

The tramp closed his eyes, swallowed and heard another sound. A second animal had appeared, a donkey, and it stood shoulder to shoulder with the bull. The new, bright star had stopped dead centre between donkey and bull and the donkey slowly knelt down on her knees. As she did so the bull calmed down and joined her in kneeling, and the tramp walked slowly out of the byre, past the notice board and into the nearest kirk, thankfully safe.

Bulls and donkeys also figure in non-travelling lore, apart from their traditional role with cattle in general. Until comparatively recently bull-baiting was quite a popular spectacle in Scotland, with a bull fastened to a stake and worried to death by a pack of dogs. Such a stake still exists in Leslie, Fife, a hefty stone on the village green, deeply scored with the chains which tethered the bull.

Bulls also had a hard time in the Highlands. In 1656 a supposedly Presbyterian area of Wester Ross was discovered sacrificing bulls to St Mourie, one of the more obscure early saints. Christianity often had to struggle hard to penetrate the muddled pagan thinking of Scotland. As elsewhere in the world.

Donkeys were not regarded highly enough to sacrifice, which must have been seen as some sort of consolation for the contempt in which they have been held down the centuries. Despised for their stupidity, maltreated for their obstinacy, only the sign of the cross displayed on their back goes in their favour. That, and also their part in an amazingly optimistic cure for whooping-cough. First the sufferer had to be passed underneath a donkey three times, followed by twice across its back. After that, a split ash was substituted for the donkey and the same pantomime repeated. Then came the clever bit – stop the next man who rode past on a piebald horse and ask what medicine he recommended.

As seems quite common in Scotland, farmyard poultry attracted both Christian and pagan lore and sometimes a curious combination of both. On St Bride's Day anyone who thought they had angered the saint buried a live cock at a spot where three burns met, a very religious site in pagan times. A cock was also maltreated to cure epilepsy, being buried alive at the place where a fit had occurred, or having its blood sprinkled over the sufferer.

Christians believed that a cock was the first creature to announce the birth at Bethlehem, and has continued to crow on Christmas Eve ever since. On Doomsday, every cock in the world, including the metal cocks posing as weathervanes on church steeples, will crow to waken the dead and alert the living.

Interestingly, the pagan Norse thought that their own doomsday – Ragnarok – would be announced by a gold-crested cock, and from the Gospels comes the idea that it was a death omen to hear a cock crow three times between sunset and midnight. A cock crowing indoors, however, meant that a stranger was coming.

In Shetland death could be avoided by greasing the wooden hinges of an outer door; this sounds like the ploy of a houseproud wife trying to make her husband do some work.

Also in Shetland was the belief that a black cock repelled fairies and trows – trolls – and so they were in great demand at births when women and babies were at their most vulnerable. Only black cocks could sense the occult presence of a trow and would crow mightily. Trows knew all about this, and chanted:

> *The white cock is nae cock*
> *Weadie, weadie,*
> *I can sit still and warm my baby*
> *The black cock is a cock*

Weadie, weadie,
I maun now flit frae warming my baby.

This does not mean that white cocks were useless. Early this century a fishing boat was lying off the south coast of Fife when a meteor hurtled toward a hay stack. Just before it landed a white cock crowed and the meteor veered away and landed in the sea. Next evening the same thing happened, with the crock crowing and the meteor splashing in the water. The seamen had watched this in wonderment and rowed ashore to buy the cock. Next night a third meteor fell, but without the crowing cock it was not diverted and landed square in the farmyard, destroying all the hay.

Where there were cocks there had to be hens, and at one time there was hardly a farm in Scotland which did not have a dozen or so hens scuttling round the steading: free-range eggs and children searching for nesting sites. Commercial egg farming came in the shape of the colony system, with rows of hen houses stretching across the fields.

Orkney specialised in this from the nineteenth century until the 1960s. In 1950 the islands exported a tremendous five million dozen eggs with just about every known species of hens contributing: Light Sussex, Rock, Leghorn, Rhode Island Red, Wyandotte – and the ubiquitous peedie hen, the Scottish bantam. In June 1952 came disaster, with a storm which wrecked thousands of irreplaceable hen houses and killed thousands of hens. Orkney fought back and egg production recovered, only to be defeated in the late 1960s and 70s by the intensive battery farming from the south.

But the hens have left their mark. Every newly-wed was once given a hen to carry into their first home: if it crowed loudly it was good luck to the marriage, but the woman would wear the trousers! On the other hand, if a hen was heard crowing like a cock it was such bad luck that it had to be destroyed. 'Whistling maids and crowing hens are no canny aboot a house,' the old proverb stated.

Sometimes hens were 'no canny' anywhere. Hen feathers created a stir in the early sixteenth century when John Damien (described as 'Maister John the French Mediciniar', but who might have been from Lombardy or even further east) came to Scotland and claimed to be first a doctor, then an alchemist. As a doctor he had purgatives that could kill a thief without using the gallows; and as an alchemist, a scientist, his frequent explosions nearly demolished Tongland Monastery.

In 1508 Maister John tried a new ploy – flying! He produced a plan for a pair of wings, tapped King James' genuine scientific enthusiasm and encouraged the collection of feathers. With hens being easily available, their feathers formed the majority in the mound which grew in Stirling, but seamen such as the Bartons and Captain Falconer also brought in swans' feathers, and commando-type raids netted feathers from the eyries of confused eagles.

John Damien leaped from the walls of Stirling Castle in September 1508 and kept going, straight down, to land in a scatter of feathers in a dung heap. Damien blamed the feathers – hens being naturally attracted to middens. Feathers from eagles would have been better. William Dunbar the poet wrote a satirical poem which put it nicely. It is called 'Ane Ballat of the False Friar of Tungland; How He Fell into the Myre Flying to Tureland'.

Damien never quite recovered his prestige in Scotland and it is unlikely he ever again stole the feathers from a hen.

NINETEEN

FISHING WITH ENCHANTED WOMEN

OF all the birds which figure in Scottish folklore, swans are given the best press. They are too large to be cute so are not loved as robins are loved, but they are consistently referred to as 'swan maidens' or 'ladies under enchantment'. Perhaps their lovely white colouring encourages this propaganda. Certainly the beliefs stretch back to Celtic times when the swan was a mystical bird.

Always seen as a bird of good fortune, if seven were found together it meant there were seven years of prosperity to come. Seven, or any multiple of seven, was a magic number to the Celts and is still regarded as lucky. As swans were devout women under enchantment, it was an evil thing to harm them and worse to kill them, especially in the Hebrides where sometimes swans and swan maidens were interchangeable.

It was summer in Islay and the Gulf Stream warmed the seas which lap round the coast of the island. On shore the hills were hazed by the heat and the sands around Loch

Gruinart shimmered like the Sahara. A lone swan flew inland and found a quiet loch, miles from human habitation. Cooled by fast flowing burns and shaded by a bracken-clad hill, the loch was too tempting to ignore and she touched gently down on the shore.

For a full minute she sat there, contemplating the beauty of Islay, then she stripped off her feather robe and slid into the loch. Soft water, cool with the slight hint of peat, only added to the charm. Time passed without the swan maiden realising it and it was nearly dark when she returned to her feather robe.

But it was gone. A young man stood where it had been, staring at her as she rose naked from the water. And suddenly she did not care about her nudity, nor did she care about the loss of her robe.

She knew he had hidden it, but she also knew that she was in love. They embraced, naturally, and within weeks they were married. It was to be a happy marriage which produced three fine, graceful children and the swan maiden nearly forgot about her previous life.

But one day her youngest and most precocious daughter found the robe. There was nothing she could do; nature demanded that the swan maiden don the robe and, with the tears salt on her cheeks she did so, cast one longing look back at her human family, and rose into the air.

For a year nothing was heard of her and her husband lived in mourning. Every day he visited the loch, but it lay empty beneath a sky which seemed perpetually grey, with the wind lifting cold ripples on the surface. Neglecting his farm, he refused to leave the area until, one year after his wife flew off, the swans returned to Islay. They flew above him, white, enchanting and untouchable, and a feather robe dropped at the water's edge. Laughing, uncaring of the consequences, he undressed, slipped on the robe and soared skyward to join his wife.

Not for centuries did he return to Islay, but when he did, and when the bells of Bowmore Kirk pealed, he crumbled to dust.

Swan maidens were a little like angels, except they needed thunder and lightning to hatch their eggs. Yet for all their supernatural qualities, they still had a human soul, so it was very bad luck to harm them. Death would follow within a year.

This mixture of mysticism and humanity enables swans to avoid the darker deeds of man, so when Cromwell's armies marched into Linlithgow and stabled their horses in the royal palace, the swans flew from Linlithgow Loch. Only with the Restoration of Charles II did the swans return. However, there is a distinct possibility that this legend was royalist propaganda.

Swans could also return good for good. There was once an old woman washing her clothes in a lochan somewhere in Benbecula. As she washed she sang, until she became aware of a faint sound nearby, like someone in pain. She investigated and discovered a swan lying injured beside the water.

With swans being nearly human and the woman being kindly by nature, she carried it home and treated its injuries, simultaneously nursing her own sick child. In wonder, she noticed that as the swan recovered strength, her child, who had been unwell for months, also began to improve. On the day the swan flapped its wings, the child sat up in bed. And on the exact minute the swan flew away, the child walked outside. By helping the swan the kindly Isleswoman had helped her own child.

One group of people who did not show much respect for the swans were the canons of Inchmahome. These were Augustine, or Black, canons and were brought to Inchmahome by Walter Comyn, Earl of Menteith in 1238. They settled on the largest island in what is now termed the Lake of Menteith. Since the arrival of the monks the island has been known as Inchmahome, but previously it was Inchmaquhomok, and could have held a Celtic monastery dedicated to St Colman.

The canons spent their time performing the work of God, attending their seven daily services and reading, gardening or fishing. Legend credits them with an interesting fishing method, whereby they took a line, baited it with a perch and tied it to the leg of a swan. When the swan swam free in the loch its rhythmic paddling motion attracted one of the pike which still frequent the loch. The pike bit at the tasty perch, the jerk stopped the swan and a tug of war developed. If the pike was small the swan took flight and disappeared; but if it was large it could hold the swan back long enough for the canons to row out and retrieve both pike and bird. Free dinner for the monks, but that was probably the only enchanted, or enchanting, woman they were ever likely to meet.

Scotland also has some interesting lore concerning geese. It was widely believed that barnacle geese were hatched from barnacles, either from rocks on the coast or from a ship's hull, and this led to the even stranger thought that geese were hatched from rotting ship's timber.

Slightly more believable is the goose which ruffles her feathers to bring snow; while a rhyme from Moray which incorporates weather lore might well be factual:

Wild geese, wild geese ganging to the sea;
Good weather it will be.
Wild geese, wild geese ganging to the hill,
The weather it will spill.

South of Harris and north of North Uist is the island of Berneray. Once it was nearly connected to Pabbay, but high tides in the sixteenth century blasted away the low sandy ground and today there is a two-mile wide channel between the two islands. Many centuries earlier, the MacAndies lived on Berneray. They were a dissatisfied clan and often watched the wild ducks which frequented the surrounding waters, envying them their freedom.

The local druid was a humane man and he called the MacAndies together and gave them a choice: stay as they were or be changed into the ducks they admired so much. A conference was held on Berneray, but the MacAndies could not decide; some wanted to become ducks but others were frightened of change and preferred the devil they knew.

'Fine,' said the druid, and flicked half of them with his magic wand. At once the MacAndies who were touched turned into wigeons and flew away, while the remainder returned to working the land. Today the wigeon still fly free over the Sound of Harris, happy MacAndies who whistle and purr their satisfaction with life and at their choice.

In their own way, they too have been enchanted.

TWENTY

ANIMALS OF THE HUNT

IT is nearly a thousand years since wild bears trampled the undergrowth in Scotland's forests and they have left behind barely a memory. Yet in their day Caledonian bears had quite a reputation for ferocity. The Romans admired them for their appearance and size and imported them for use in appalling ritual executions. No doubt there was native help in rounding up the bears, unless the Romans sent out very heavily-guarded hunting expeditions. In either case this must have been one of Scotland's earliest exports.

When the bears reached the Empire, and the percentage which survived the journey was probably quite small, they were let loose on some unfortunate rascal who happened to be disliked by the authorities. This happened in the Coliseum or similar amphitheatre and the victim was handicapped by being tied naked to a cross. A fine sporting spectacle.

Bears survived in Scotland for 700 years after the Romans left, but they were good eating and provided excellent winter coats, so by the twelfth century they were extinct. The hunters had to search for alternative game.

If they were lucky they might have found reindeer. These great animals, among the earliest to be domesticated, wandered Scotland from Kyle to Caithness and were contemporary with both the woolly mammoth and shaggy Viking – which means they have lived in Scotland far longer than the Scots. The Norse Earls of Orkney used to cross to Caithness to hunt both reindeer and red deer. Caithness was firmly within the Norse orbit and so the wild moorland was in effect a private hunting ground for the Earls.

By this period a gradual climatic warming was forcing the reindeer north and only one is featured on a stone carving in Speyside; they were on their way out. Perhaps the climate killed them, or the hunters, but they vanished for hundreds of years, to be re-introduced in the middle of the twentieth century by the British Reindeer Company and Mikel Utsi, a Lapp. Perhaps surprisingly, they thrive.

As do red deer. Once creatures of the forests, they have adapted well to the bare Highland hills and if not culled would over-breed and possibly starve. Since the last wolf has long gone from Scotland, there are no real natural enemies for mature deer, except man. Although, if man is an enemy, man is also a benefactor – for the present deer forests sit squarely on land once used for pasturing cattle. Deer were considered more profitable, so the landlords evicted the sitting native population and now deer are farmed, bred for the hunter's rifle. The wilderness is nothing less than a succession of huge deer farms.

It was not always so. Once the deer were

milked by the fairies who sang enchanting melodies to keep them quiet. This is not as unbelievable as it sounds: Seton Gordon, the great naturalist, was once in a Cairngorm bothy when he played the pipes and a herd of stags came from the hill to dance on their hind legs. Deer must be partial to music.

And deer milk was seemingly popular in the old days, with heroes like Cuchillan the hound drinking it in quantity to keep up his strength. He hunted the deer too; in one legendary hunt in Skye he bagged six thousand.

With the vast acreages of sporting estates spreading across the Highlands during the nineteenth century, and the consequent removal of the people to the coasts and overseas, the stalker came into his own. Not so much a deer hunter as a deer herder, the stalker brings the weekend sportsman to his prey, instructs him how and when to shoot and deals with the messy aftermath.

Stalkers are the true deer experts. They know that deer can be 'cliffed' by golden eagles, which means the eagle dives on the deer and uses its huge wings to drive a victim over a precipice to its death below. This provides a meal for the eagle.

Some stalkers even have the ability to approach a sleeping deer and touch it. They all know that a herd – a stag and his hinds – is rarely silent with the stag muttering to himself and a hind yelping a warning from time to time. Sometimes the deer encounter unnatural hazards, entangle their antlers in barbed wire and have to be helped, or shot. This is the stalker's task, and it is a hard task with a distinctive language.

A male deer in his first year of life is known as a 'knobber', next year he is a 'brocket', and in his third, when a brow antler appears, he is a 'spayard'. During his fourth year a bay antler comes and he is known as a 'staggard'; and only when the royal antlers grow in his fifth year does he become a stag. After that he could become a stag of ten, or, if he survives a royal hunt, a stag royal.

It was a stag royal which was the cause of the founding of Holyrood Abbey in the twelfth century. One Sunday, against the wishes of his priests, King David was hunting a mile or so from the castle in Edinburgh when he became separated from the rest of his party. Dismounting to drink from a spring, he realised that a large stag with a full set of extremely sharp antlers was watching him. And rather than the king hunting the deer, the deer was prepared to hunt its king as it swept sideways with his horns and knocked David off his feet.

Lying on the ground, David saw the deer poised above him and realised that he should not have ridden to hunt on a Sunday. With sudden inspiration – or in sheer panic – he held up the crucifix he wore to fend off the beast. At once the stag reared up and retreated to the woods.

In gratitude for his deliverance, David founded an abbey – the Abbey of the Holy Rood, or cross – the ruins of which still stand behind the palace of Holyroodhouse in Edinburgh. Often mispronounced 'Holly Rood', the abbey's origin is remembered by the stag's head with a cross between the antlers which decorates both the gates of the palace and the Canongate Kirk.

Deer were also hunted in the hill forests of the border, notably the Ettrick Forest. It was here that Thomas Learmonth, usually termed 'Thomas the Rhymer', was recalled to fairyland where he had already spent seven years. The messengers came in the shape of a hart and a hind, who walked quietly down the main street of Ercildoune, now Earlston.

Deer still wander into the streets of border towns. Only a few years back Brian Romanes was driving into Galashiels from Selkirk when he met a roe deer running along the road. Rather than run away, the deer turned toward him and, timing its leap to perfection, jumped over his moving car and escaped unhurt.

Seldom thought of as a beast of the chase, the wild white cattle of Scotland (*Urus scoticus*) were hunted for centuries. It is believed that these White Park Cattle were brought in by the Romans and turned wild when the legions departed; although it is also possible that the breed is older and was the original species of cattle back in Paleolithic times.

Either way they were enclosed into hunting parks in the thirteenth century and were chased by, among others, Robert The Bruce and James IV. Both kings hunted the Cadzow herds in Lanarkshire, the descendants of which still, thankfully, exist.

Of all the animals regularly hunted in Scotland, the most feared is also the smallest – the hare. This animal could not rend people with claws like the bear, it had no clashing teeth like the wolf, no antlers like the deer nor tusks like the boar. Instead it had … superstition. For the hare was as likely as not to be a witch.

There are many tales of hares being wounded in a hunt, only for the hunter to hear of an old woman with an unaccountable injury. To ensure that a hare was in fact only an animal, it was advisable to shoot it with a silver bullet, or an arrow barbed with silver, for then it would change into its true shape. Or not, as the case may be.

Known as a 'bawd' in Lowland Scotland, for a hare to cross someone's path was so ill-omened that it was better to return home and stay there. If a pregnant woman met one, her child would be born with a hare lip; and if a fisherman met one, he would have bad luck and empty nets.

Possibly the worst bringer of bad luck was

the hare which burst in on King James IV's council of war in September 1513. Jinking and weaving, it avoided the hundreds of missiles which were hurled at it by the assembled army, to vanish into the whispering grass of Northumberland. The Scottish army marched on to the terrible defeat of Flodden Field.

Rather than transform themselves into hares, sometimes witches used hares in their own spells. In the middle ages there were rumours of a lamp which, when burning, made all women present strip off their clothes and dance until the fuel was consumed. The fuel was hare fat!

EPILOGUE

THEY are still there, these animals – in our streets and our stories and our imaginations. They have lived with us for millennia and it is somehow comforting to know we still have them. If wolves and bears have gone from our forests, we are the safer for that, and we still have deer roaming free. Few people today admit to having seen a water horse, but monster hunters thrive by Loch Ness and there are occasional sightings of unusual beasts throughout Scotland ... and elsewhere.

Our farms still contain sheep and cattle, horses are as popular as ever, dogs remain as faithful as always, and cats just as enigmatic. Which is all as it should be.

Industrialisation and urban living have put a veneer on us all – but beneath this the call of an unknown animal in the night can still raise the hairs on the back of our necks. The sight of a scurrying spider still panics many. Superstition is never far away, folk memories remain, and for that reason – and for their sheer entertainment – folk stories and folklore will never die.

BIBLIOGRAPHY

Brown, R Lamont: *Scottish Superstitions* (Edinburgh: W & R Chambers Ltd, 1990).

Gray, Affleck: *Legends of the Cairngorms* (Edinburgh: Mainstream Publishing, 1987).

MacGregor, Alasdair Alpin: *The Western Isles* (London: Robert Hale, 1949).

Marwick, Ernest W: *The Folklore of Orkney and Shetland* (Batsford, 1986).

Radford: *Superstitions of the Countryside* (London: Arrow, 1979).

Thompson, Francis: *A Scottish Bestiary* (Molendinar Press, 1978).

Williamson: *Fireside Tales of the Traveller Children* (Edinburgh: Canongate Publishing, 1995).